MORE FOOD FOR LESS SPACE!

There are few households which cannot
produce at least some of their own food
requirements. You don't even need a
garden – it's astonishing what has been
achieved with the bare minimum of space.
In *Home-Grown Food*, Roy Genders, who
is the author of many books on gardening,
including two volumes for the *Pears
Encyclopaedia* series, describes how to grow
an enormous variety of vegetables in tubs
and windowboxes, up walls and trellises,
on kitchen windowsills, and even under
stairs. This is a book which will give
practical advice and a great deal of pleasure
to everyone who is short of space yet wants
to grow their own produce.

Home-Grown Food

A Guide for Town Gardeners

ROY GENDERS

SPHERE BOOKS LIMITED
30/32 Gray's Inn Road, London WC1X 8JL

First published in Great Britain by
Michael Joseph Ltd. 1976
Copyright © Roy Genders 1976
First Sphere Books edition 1978

Set in Monotype Bembo

Printed in Great Britain by
C. Nicholls & Company Ltd
The Philips Park Press, Manchester

CONTENTS

ILLUSTRATIONS

CHAPTER ONE

WHERE FOOD CAN BE GROWN

At no time in our history, except perhaps during the two World Wars, has it seemed to be of greater importance to produce as much of our own food as possible than today. Not only is this necessary to combat the ever-rising cost of living in this inflationary age but there may come a time when the country will no longer be able to import all the food its people needs, primarily owing to our being unable to pay for it. It will then be a matter of feeding ourselves to a large extent, yet the farmer and market gardener will be able to grow only a small part of our requirements. It will be necessary to utilize the garden and allotment to maximum advantage and it will be up to each of us to explore every place available which can be utilized for food growing. For many people, including the self-employed who do not have the backing of a powerful union to ensure that their income keeps up with the cost of living, and those whose only income is their pension – rising prices are a continual worry and these are the people now to be seen digging their gardens at weekends and after a hard day's work has been done, to ensure that at least a proportion of the fresh food they eat will be grown for the minimum cost. All that is necessary is a few packets of seed and a small amount of manure and fertilizer, their cost being infinitesimal when compared with that of vegetables purchased from the greengrocer or from the deep freeze in the supermarket. 'Grow Your Own' should now be the aim of every able-bodied person.

From a piece of ground no more than 20 ft. by 15 ft. which is usually available with the smallest of houses, it is possible to produce most of one's vegetable requirements for the whole of the year, concentrating on those crops which make the most economic use of the ground and which will crop over the longest possible time. Potatoes, still reasonably priced for the amount of nourishment they provide, can be obtained from a wholesaler or farmer (preferably when they are lifted in late autumn) and, if correctly stored away from frost and in the dark, they will keep sound all winter. As the winter advances, potatoes become dearer owing to their additional handling and greater scarcity so it pays to purchase the bulk of one's requirements in autumn when they are usually dry at lifting time and so keep better.

A well-stocked deep freeze unit will also achieve a considerable saving and will provide a meal at any time of the day or night without the need to visit the shops. The saving on petrol alone is considerable and the food is always there in a fresh condition when required.

An inexpensive method of filling the freezer is to purchase fresh vegetables such as runner beans, cauliflowers, broccoli and Brussels sprouts from local allotment gardeners and market growers when the crops are in fresh condition and in summer time when at their cheapest. Cauliflowers and beans must be marketed as soon as they reach maturity; when they are in full season the grower will accept whatever price he can get and that is the time to buy for the freezer.

Cabbages and savoys, swedes and turnips, which are too bulky to put in the freezer, can stay in the home garden to be used fresh as required all through the year. But in summer there may also be surplus cauliflowers, broccoli, Brussels sprouts and beans which can be put in the freezer, so that these delicacies are available throughout winter and there should be no vegetables which go to seed and are wasted. Where the freezer can be used as a complement to the garden, then one may be sure of obtaining the maximum value for one's outlay and labours.

Those with no garden but who may have a small courtyard or balcony adjoining their home can still grow excellent crops of both fruit and vegetables, including a number of luxury crops whose current price in the shops puts them out of range of all but those of the higher income groups. Even tomatoes are now in the luxury class, whereas until recent times they were obtainable for a shilling a pound during the summer and few troubled to grow them apart from market gardeners. Today, even at the height of the season, home-grown tomatoes will cost 20p. per lb. and considerably more during the early weeks of summer. A greenhouse is not essential to grow heavy crops of this popular food – though with a greenhouse, earlier crops can be obtained.

A greenhouse will be useful for many additional ways of growing food such as the raising of vegetable plants, especially those which need to be sown early as they require a long season to mature, whilst several crops besides tomatoes will grow well if given the warmth and protection of glass or plastic sheeting. A small greenhouse can be erected in any suitably sized courtyard which receives an average amount of sunlight and, properly maintained, will give years of service for a modest capital outlay.

A cold frame, too, can be placed in a courtyard as an alternative to a greenhouse, or as an addition to it, and here may be grown marrows and melons, cucumbers and tomatoes, planting them in pots where there is no soil.

SUITABLE SITUATIONS

Against the sunny wall of a courtyard, tomatoes can be grown in pots or boxes, the plants being supported by canes fastened to wires stretched across the wall; or a vine may be grown, and blackberries on the shady side. These plants will hide an unsightly wall during the summer months and provide delicious fruit in autumn.

Cordon apples and espalier pears can be grown on a sunny wall where the fruit will ripen before the frosts so long as they are planted in deep boxes or large pots. Dessert gooseberries, too, will do well under similar conditions but may also be grown in cordon form against a wall which receives only a limited amount of sunlight. Tubs arranged around a courtyard or on a verandah may be made colourful in summer with bush tomatoes. A suitable variety is Pixie. Plant amongst them one or two geraniums, edging the tubs with blue trailing lobelia. The combination of colours is most attractive, the brilliant scarlet of the tomatoes and the bright green leaves matching the similar colourings of the geraniums, whilst the latter provide protection from winds and late frosts.

Barrels in which holes of 1 in. diameter have been drilled and which are then filled with soil are suitable for planting with strawberries, or the runners can be set around the edge of tubs with tomatoes at the centre. They need some sun to ripen the fruits but strawberries do well in the partial shade of other plants.

Use can be made of wooden trellis to hide unsightly dustbins or an outside coal bunker, for the trellis may be made to yield a heavy crop of runner beans or blackberries which at the same time will cover the trellis with handsome foliage during the summer months. Trellis can also be used to divide one part of the garden from another, possibly where vegetables are grown at one end of the garden and here too, the trellis should be used to support food crops.

Rustic poles may be used as an alternative and are attractive where erected on either side of a path and so constructed as to form a type of pergola. The Oregon thornless blackberry, delicious in fruit and handsome in leaf, will be ideal to clothe the poles; or use the Japanese wineberry with its crimson canes in winter – the fruit makes an excellent conserve.

THE NUTRITIONAL VALUE OF FRESH VEGETABLES

A garden shed, so useful for storing a bicycle and one's tools as well as all manner of garden requisites, can also be used to grow food crops. Chicory and seakale can be forced under the bench and a crop of mushrooms grown in boxes or in floor beds. Rhubarb, too, can be brought inside for winter forcing, whilst on top of the bench by a window (for they need light), potatoes may be 'chitted' (sprouted) to give earlier and heavier crops. Mustard and cress can be grown in boxes or on flannel or felt, as it also can be in the kitchen window. Here, too, alfalfa seed, one of the world's wonder foods so rich in life-giving amino-acids, can be grown in a similar way; also Chinese Mung beans and fenugreek with their high protein content and abundance of vitamins and iron.

There are many wonderful edible plants that can be grown in the window of a warm room which will add interest and vitamins to a summer or winter salad. All that is necessary is to place the seeds in a shallow, waterproof container as used in a freezer and to keep the seed moist. To start them off, place them in a warm, dark cupboard and when the seed begins to sprout, move to a window sill. It is said that the food value of seed is increased by more than five hundred per cent when it is sprouting for it is then far richer in protein, which accounts for twenty per cent of our body weight and which is present in our muscles, hair, skin and bones, and we constantly need fresh supplies to replace that which is used up in the formation of those parts of the body.

Protein is comprised of twenty-two amino-acids, eight of which the body is unable to manufacture itself. These have to be supplied in the form of those foods which are rich in protein such as the soya or vegetable bean and sprouted seeds which, together with home-grown green vegetables, will provide the body with all that is necessary to maintain it in good condition and enable it to fight disease. Even where there is no garden, the essential plant foods can be grown.

Besides the garden shed, use can be made of a garage, often heated in winter, to grow mushrooms in boxes stacked around the sides. An outhouse, built of stone or brick and usually quite warm in winter, will be equally suitable and here, too, rhubarb can be forced; also seakale and chicory, the succulent stems providing valuable protein when used raw in a salad or making delicious eating when cooked. These foods can be used in place of the now expensive meat dishes or to replace at least a part of our meat diet, and our meals will be equally nutritious and satisfying.

For those past the age of fifty, home-grown foods and sprouted seeds can entirely replace meats with gratifying results. Professor Cheeke, for example, working with alfalfa at the State University, Oregon, has found that the sprouted seed contains valuable cholesterol-reducing agents. This he discovered when feeding quantities to animals, their blood and tissue levels of cholesterol — the greatest cause of heart disease — being much reduced. In a room temperature of 68°F. (20°C.) alfalfa seed will germinate in five days, and every few hours doubles in weight. After four days, vitamin B^2 in the growing 'sprouts' will have increased by more than one thousand per cent, and this is the vitamin needed to combat dandruff and eczema and other skin troubles. Riboflavin, which is the technical term for this vitamin food, is present also in the leaves of dandelion, lettuce and nasturtium which can readily be grown in a window box.

'Vitamin' became an important word in our language in 1912. It is derived from the Latin *vita*, life, but the discovery of what were originally known as 'accessory food substances' took place some thirty years earlier, though it is only in the last quarter of a century that their importance in the diet has become fully appreciated.

Vitamin A (carotene) is needed for healthy bone and tissue growth, especially for young children, and in vegetables it is provided particularly by the leaves of dandelion and spinach, also by those of parsley and mustard and cress which is readily grown on the kitchen windowsill for sandwiches and salads. They also provide the body with vitamin C which protects against the common cold and keeps the blood vessels in a healthy condition. Sprouted alfalfa is also rich in vitamin C.

Vitamin B¹ (thiamin) is provided by dried peas and beans which can be stored in boxes or jars to use through winter. This is the vitamin needed for the digestive and nervous systems. Peas and beans also provide the body with vitamin B⁶ which promotes the healing of body tissue after injury or operation.

Vitamin E (tocopherol) is the important heart vitamin, present also in dried peas and beans and in most green vegetables, which should be put through the 'juicer' to mix with apple or citrus juice for a health-giving cocktail to start the day.

Grapes and peppers in particular, both readily grown in a greenhouse or against the wall of a sunny courtyard, will provide the body with vitamin C, necessary to maintain the correct flow of blood through the arteries and veins. And to prevent haemorrhage, cress, nasturtium and dandelion leaves eaten raw as well as cabbage, kale and Brussels sprouts lightly cooked will provide the body with vitamin K.

To be most effective, all fruits, vegetables and herbs should be used fresh. By growing one's own, it is possible to have nasturtium leaves all through summer, and cress and dandelion leaves (forced under cloches) all the year round, for use in salads as a welcome addition to lettuce.

Vegetables and their vitamin content:

Vegetable				Vitamins			
Bean (Green)	A	B^1	B^2		C		
Beetroot	A				C		
Brussels sprouts	A	B^1		B^6	C		K
Cabbage and Kale	A	B^1	BB^2	B^6	C		
Carrot	A	B^1	B^2	B^6	C	E	
Cauliflower and Broccoli	A	B^1	B^2	B^6	C		
Courgette		B^1		B^6	C	E	
Cucumber		B^1	B^2		C		
Dandelion	A		B^2		C	E	K
Lettuce	A	B^1	B^2	B^6	C	E	
Melon	A	B^1	B^2	B^6	C		
Mustard and Cress	A		B^2		C	E	
Onion		B^1	B^2	B^6	C		
Parsley	A		B^2		C		
Pea	A	B^1	B^2		C		
Pepper				B^6	C		
Radish	A	B^1	B^2	B^6	C		
Spinach	A				C	E	K
Sweet Corn	A				C		
Tomato	A				C		K
Watercress	A				C	E	K

In addition to vitamins, the body requires mineral salts, especially iron, calcium and phosphates, to enable it to function correctly. And in the same way that soil, well supplied with plant food, is unable to release these foods unless lime is present, so too is the body unable to make full use of the vitamins unless mineral salts are also present. The two go hand-in-hand in the maintenance of a healthy body.

Tomatoes and peppers are rich in potassium salts and iron whereas calcium is present only in green vegetables, whether eaten raw or lightly cooked. They should be cooked in as little water as possible, or ideally simmered in their own juices. Never add bicarbonate of soda to the water for this will destroy every vitamin. Steaming will add a new interest to most green vegetables, retaining their maximum flavour and vitamin value.

GROWING FOOD WITHOUT A GARDEN

Many of the most health-giving of all vegetables may be grown where there is no garden at all. Nasturtiums can be sown in hanging baskets suspended from the wall of a house or courtyard where they provide a splash of colour with their scarlet and yellow flowers all summer as well as vitamins from their leaves. After the flowers fade, the seeds can be pickled while still green and used as a substitute for capers. The trailing Gleam varieties are most suitable for hanging baskets. Simply press six seeds into the compost around the edge of the basket. If you wish, plant a scarlet geranium in the centre of each basket and around it set marjoram, hyssop and chives to use for flavouring all the year round. And if two or three plants of trailing *Nepeta* (alehoof) are set at the edge with the nasturtiums, the baskets will remain green all the year. When the nasturtiums die back in late autumn, pull them out and save the seeds for pickling, fresh seed being planted in April the following year.

Window-boxes can be utilized in the same way; or build a low retaining wall 15-18 in. from the sun-drenched wall of a courtyard or the wall of an outhouse, to a height of 18 in., fill the space between with compost and plant marrows and ridge cucumbers which will trail over the sides. Tomatoes or climbing beans planted at the back will cover a wall with their luxuriant foliage which should be supported by trellis, wires or canes. Orange boxes of similar size and placed alongside each other at the bottom of a wall may be painted white or green on the outside and planted with similar food plants.

Small boxes 6-8 in. deep can be fixed at varying heights to the walls of a courtyard by means of strong brackets and planted with dwarf herbs such as marjoram, winter savory, parsley and chives, to be used for flavouring omelettes, soups and stews throughout the year. Again, a few nasturtium seeds can be planted at the front so they will hide any unsightliness of the retaining wall or the boxes during summer as well as providing, with their leaves, a much appreciated addition to the salad bowl.

Indeed, every bare wall should be made to produce its quota of food and every outbuilding, shed and cellar made to grow enjoyable out-of-season dishes, health-giving foods for only a fraction of their cost in shops. They will take up very little of one's leisure, the work being done in the evenings and at weekends, the plants requiring only an occasional watering at other times.

Where there is a strip of poor soil in full sun, perhaps beneath the wall of the house where annuals are usually sown for summer flowering, herbs which like dry conditions can be grown. When in flower, they will attract butterflies and bees from afar and will be a source of interest all year. Not only should the culinary herbs be planted – the sages, thymes and marjoram – but also those that give pleasure in other ways; to use in potpourris and sweet bags to place amongst clothes, and to add to a bath of warm water to refresh the tired limbs. Their culture is very simple for they will flourish in a poor soil as long as it is well-drained in winter and they can feel the sun's rays in summer to bring out the full fragrance of their leaves. A herb garden is a never-ending source of delight throughout the year.

VEGETABLES FOR FREEZING

The use of a deep freezing unit in conjunction with the production of one's own vegetables will not only make possible the preserving of fruits and vegetables when at their best, but it will mean that there is no wastage. How often has it happened in the past that with no freezer, cauliflowers and broccoli could not all be used when reaching their best and so quickly ran to seed. With a freezer, the curds can be removed and placed in the unit as they reach perfection, to be enjoyed, still in peak condition, through the winter when outside crops are expensive. This may be due to there being few fresh vegetables about owing to the severity of the weather, or perhaps after a long dry summer when field-grown plants made little growth.

It may be that one is able to use all the crops, each in its season, apart from storing a few onions and some potatoes. If this is so, obtain all the fresh vegetables throughout the year when they are reasonably priced and put them in the freezer to use when they are most expensive. Always keep the freezer filled, for the less air space there is, the less current it needs to maintain the correct temperature.

Remember, whether growing and freezing one's own vegetables or buying them in their season, always freeze the crop when at its best. Peas and beans left too long on the plant will have become hard and devoid of flavour and freezing will not improve them, whilst beetroot and carrots, both of which freeze admirably, will become hard and woody and virtually uneatable if left too long in the ground. Grow the crops well, keeping them supplied with moisture during dry weather, and harvest each in turn as it reaches its peak.

Almost all vegetables freeze well but so important has the freezer become in the economy of the household that the hybridizers are now concentrating on the introduction of varieties that behave particularly well when frozen. With dwarf beans, for example, both the new Processor and older Masterpiece freeze to perfection, and in carrots, Sweetheart and Chantenay Red Core are especially suitable, being better than all others as they have been raised to produce a root in which the core is of the same colour and softness as the main stem.

These vegetables are very suitable for freezing:

Vegetable	Variety	Sow	Harvest
Bean, broad	Imperial Green	October	June
„	The Sutton	March	July
Bean, dwarf	Masterpiece	May-June	August
„	Processor	May-June	August
„	Remus	May-June	August
Bean, runner	Crusader	May	August-September
„	Kelvedon Marvel	May	August-September
Beetroot	Detroit Globe	May	August-September
„	Early Model	May	August-September
Borecole (Kale)	Dwarf Green Curled	March	August-October
Broccoli, large heading	Newton Seale	April	April-May
	St. Agnes	April	December-January
Broccoli, sprouting	Early Purple	April	October-December
	White Star Perennial	April	February-May
Brussels sprouts	Peer Gynt	April	October-December
„	Sigmund	April	January-March
Calabrese	Green Comet	April	October-December
Carrot	Chantenay Red Core	April	August-October
„	Juwarot	April	August-October
Cauliflower	Delta	April	August-September
„	Snow King	April	July-August
Pea	Early Onward	April	July
„	Kelvedon Wonder	April	Late July
„	Hurst's Green Shaft	April	Early August
Spinach	Monarch	March-May	July-September

There are other varieties, a number of which are equally good for freezing, but those mentioned have been tried and found to be excellent, keeping in condition for at least a year or more.

In fruits: blackberries, loganberries, gooseberries and rhubarb will freeze well, retaining their shape and their good eating qualities for at least a year. As with vegetables, freeze them as soon as possible after gathering, certainly on the same day and preferably within an hour or so, before they begin to go 'mushy'. Blackberries and strawberries, especially, should be gathered on the point of ripeness otherwise they will become too soft to freeze well.

Fruits do not need blanching before placing in the freezer, but vegetables do. As with fruits, blanch vegetables as soon after picking as possible. Blanching is the operation of scalding the vegetables in boiling water for several minutes before placing them in thin polythene bags and consigning to the freezer. This scalding is to render the enzymes in the cells inactive, so that colour, quality and flavour are fully retained whilst frozen, and when thawed the vegetables are in exactly the same condition as before.

Place the vegetables in a fine-mesh wire basket after preparing them as for table: topping and tailing and slicing runner beans, shelling peas, cleaning and slicing carrots, though small ones may be left whole. Cauliflowers and broccoli are broken into small bunches or pieces with about 2 in. of stem attached. In this way the vegetables are more easily blanched whilst they are fully prepared for serving when thawed. Also when cut up, they take up less space in the freezer.

The basket with the vegetables is placed in a pan containing five to six pints of water for each pound of vegetables, with a little salt added. The water is brought to the boil so that the vegetables are partially cooked and they remain immersed for one to five minutes depending upon the variety, broad beans taking fully five minutes before they are blanched. It is important to time the blanching from the moment the vegetables enter the boiling water or from when the water comes to the boil. If blanched too long, the eating and keeping qualities will be impaired. At exactly the right time, lift out the basket and immerse in cold water for the same number of minutes to cool. Then drain off and place in polythene bags which are tightly closed with plastic-covered ties; or the vegetables may be placed in plastic containers with a tightly fitting lid, for it is important that the vegetables (and fruits) do not become dehydrated through moisture evaporation when in the freezer. Place in the coldest part of the freezer for twenty-four hours, or lower the temperature so that the newly-added food is frozen as quickly as possible. The temperature is then increased to that of normal running.

Apart from sweet corn which is completely thawed before cooking, thawing is not necessary for vegetables. Just empty the pack and boil as required. These are the blanching times for vegetables:

Vegetable	Minutes	Method
Bean, broad	5-6	Remove from pods
Bean, dwarf	3-4	Top, tail and slice
Bean, runner	5	Remove string and slice
Beetroot	Until tender	Remove tops
Borecole (Kale)	3-4	Use young shoots
Broccoli, sprouting	4-5	Remove excess stem
Brussels sprouts	5-6	Remove outer leaves
Calabrese	4-5	Remove excess stem
Carrot	5	Slice into rings
Cauliflower	4-5	Remove stems
Parsley	3	Make into small bunches
Peas	2	Remove from pods
Rhubarb	—	Cut into 1 in. pieces
Spinach	3-4	Use only young leaves
Sweet Corn	5-6	Remove husk and stem

Cabbages and savoys are not suitable for freezing and in any case will stand out through the coldest weather unharmed, whilst potatoes (although they can be blanched for five to six minutes and will freeze well) and most root crops will store perfectly well in boxes of sand and should not take up valuable space in the freezer which is better used for the more choice crops. It should be said that tomatoes will freeze, but upon thawing usually turn 'mushy' and are suitable only for making tomato soup and to add their flavour to stews.

Fruits do not need blanching. Pick them dry and place in the freezer at once, after putting them in polythene bags or airtight containers. Strawberries should be placed singly on a sheet of cardboard and placed in this manner in the freezer for two hours until frozen solid. Over-ripe fruits should not be used. They are then placed in polythene bags before putting back in the freezer and will remain entirely separate when thawed, without going into 'mush'. To defrost fruits, place in a refrigerator for five to six hours to thaw slowly, before serving. Sugar to one's taste can be added either then or when the fruits are placed in the freezer.

After twelve months, the freezer will need defrosting and it is advisable to have it serviced every year. Insure against any loss which might follow a power cut. Any of the top insurance companies will do this.

CHAPTER TWO

FOOD FROM WALLS

Every house has a wall even if it has no garden and, in addition, many town houses have walls surrounding the courtyard or back-yard as it is usually called. Here, the walls will be enhanced by covering them with plants which will, in addition to their beauty, grow a valuable food crop. Where there is no soil, this may be overcome by building an 18 in. high retaining wall at the base of a sunny wall, using the same materials of which the wall was built. Second-hand bricks are obtainable from most demolition sites merely for their taking and a handyman will be able to erect a low retaining wall using a bag of cement and some sand. Stones, also obtainable from an old outhouse or wall may be used in like manner; or simulated stone, such as the Cotswold blocks manufactured by Bradley Products of Swindon and supplied by most builders' merchants, will make a wall of pleasing effect. If cheapness is the criterion, then use three courses (three rows) of breeze blocks also obtainable from builders' merchants. They may be camouflaged by placing on top or at the base long narrow window-boxes which may be filled with flowers or, better still, with food crops. Retaining walls should not be built against the walls of a house, except perhaps at the side, as this would encourage dampness in the house.

MAKING A WALL

Cotswold blocks have the appearance of Cotswold stone but as they are made to one size, it is an easy matter for even the inexperienced handyman to erect a low wall in fairly quick time. A low wall filled with an earth core and built about 18 in. high may be erected so as to divide one part of the garden from another. Here, too, may be grown the more compact herbs and other plants such as French beans, lettuce and chives with the health-giving nasturtium trailing over the stone which will be enhanced by the brilliance of its flowers.

Where a low wall is being made directly on to a solid base there will be no need to make a concrete foundation, though this should be done before erecting a wall over a soil base. All that is necessary is to place a thick layer of cement over the base (usually asphalt or concrete) and to press the bricks or stones into it and continue in this way, layer by layer, until the wall is built to the required height. Use a line on the outer edge to keep the wall straight, moving it up with each course, whilst the use of a builder's level will enable the wall to be kept horizontal throughout. Greater strength will be obtained if the stones (or bricks) are placed so that the second layer covers the points where the lower layer is cemented and so on throughout. A bricklayer's trowel will enable the work to be done as quickly as possible.

Where a wall is built to divide the garden, the wall will have two sides, which should be complementary to each other, and a central core. As the work progresses, it is advisable to put in the core when once the cement has set hard. At the base, add a 2 in. layer of broken brick or shingle for drainage, then begin adding the compost — made up of fresh loam which is preferable to the old soil of a town garden — and mix with it moist peat and coarse sand in the proportion of two parts loam, one part each peat, sand and decayed manure. This will consolidate as the wall is built and will therefore need topping up about a week after the wall is finished before any planting can be done.

It is important to have the cement of the right consistency; it should be neither sloppy nor too dry. Make a circle of sand on a board about 2-3 ft. square, place some cement inside and add water, turning the sand and cement until the whole is well mixed and in the right condition for easy spreading. About one part cement should be used to four parts of sand and do not mix it until required. It must then be used as quickly as possible, before it begins to set hard.

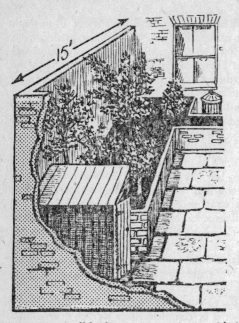

Retaining wall built around a courtyard.

A stone wall looks most attractive on either side of a stone arch used as an entrance to the vegetable garden. The walls need be no more than 2 ft. high and they lend character to any garden if planted with one of the compact lavenders, *l. nana compacta* or Folgate Blue which grows 15 in. tall, or with culinary herbs, with the ground beyond the wall reserved for vegetables.

A retaining wall around a courtyard or possibly at the base of a sunny wall should be built about 18 in. from the wall and the same in height. This will give the plants a sufficient depth of soil to promote vigorous and healthy growth with the roots not too restricted. If it is not possible to build a wall, plants may still be grown there by using window-boxes (see Chapter 3) or orange boxes placed end to end. They may be painted white or green and if used only for tomatoes, runner beans, or other annual food plants, may be emptied at the end of October and the boxes stored. This will preserve them and they will not look unsightly during winter. Boxes to be used for tomatoes should be filled with a compost made up of two parts turf loam and one part each peat and decayed manure. The boxes, obtainable from greengrocers for a few pence each, will be about 15 in. deep and capable of growing a good crop of tomatoes (or beans). The plants can be grown at the back of the boxes close to the wall and lettuce planted near the front which will have matured before the tomato plants have grown large. Radishes and spring onions can also be sown.

Much the same may be said about filling the space between the wall and a newly built retaining wall, but here there should be a 3-in. layer of crushed brick to allow surplus moisture to drain away. This may be necessary following a summer storm which is so often accompanied by a cloud-burst or following prolonged winter rain, and to add drainage a 1-in. space should be provided at intervals of about 4 ft. between the stones of the first course.

In spring two ounces of bone meal or steamed bone flour per yard should be forked into the top 6 in. of soil, which will release its plant food over a long period. Also at this time, give a one ounce per yard dressing of superphosphate to encourage root action, and one ounce of sulphate of potash which will assist the ripening of the tomatoes and enhance the colour and quality. These fertilizers should be forked into the surface at planting time.

SUPPORTING WALL PLANTS

Permanent wall plants such as vines and figs and the ornamental-leaved hybrid berries, also plums and pears, will require supporting, the shoots being trained and tied in as they form. A wooden trellis is the best way to support wall plants, the trellis being made of laths 1 in. wide and half an inch thick. They are made into 12 in. squares and fastened to the wall by plugging it with wood which slightly protrudes. The frame is screwed or nailed to the plugs so that it is about 1 in. from the wall and, in this way, the stems of the plants have room to intertwine. The frame should be fixed about 3 in. above soil level so that the lower laths are not in contact with the soil. It will have a longer life and look less conspicuous if it is creosoted before being fixed and this should be done a month before the plants are to be tied in.

Nu-Frame lattice panels are a suitable alternative. They are constructed from rigid PVC laths secured at their pivot points with tubular plastic rivets. This gives added strength and provides location points for fixing. The material is strong yet light to handle and is rot-proof, neither will it split nor warp. It is obtainable in either diamond or square pattern in 6 ft. by 2 ft. sections.

Auriol trellis, made of welded steel with a plastic finish in green or white will also give lasting support. A six-bar trellis will be 2 ft. 6 in. wide, each 'window' being 10 in. by 5 in.

Another way of supporting wall plants is by means of strong galvanized wire which is threaded through special nails containing an 'eye' which protrudes about an inch from the wall. The nails should be fixed in rows about 18 in. above each other and 4 ft. apart. The best method is to begin near the top of the wall and to continue the wiring all the way down to the base in this manner.

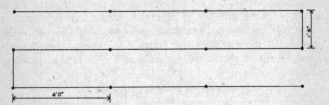

In this way, the wire may be pulled taut and, if necessary, tightened at a later date without inserting more nails. This method will be ideal for blackberries and hybrid berries. The wire will soon lose its brightness and become quite inconspicuous.

Yet another method of giving support is to fix Netlon plastic netting to a wall by means of hooks fixed to the wall by plugs. The netting is supplied in rolls 20 ft. long by 18 in. wide and is of 2 in. square mesh. It is obtainable in either green or woodtan and looks especially attractive against a wall which has been treated with Snowcem. It will in any case soon be hidden by the foliage of the plants and is as durable as trellis or galvanized wire.

It is important to make a good beginning in giving support to wall plants and one's original outlay will last for many years, producing heavy crops year after year whilst at the same time beautifying an unexciting courtyard with handsome foliage.

Wooden trellis in square or diamond shape may also be used and erected away from a wall to grow vines, hybrid berries, runner beans and other food plants needing support. The trellis may be erected to a height of 6–8 ft. so as to hide an unsightly dustbin, shed or coal bunker situated in a corner of a yard or garden. So that the trellis will not be blown over by strong winds, it should be held in place by 2 in. square timbers driven well into the ground and preferably cemented in. If it is to be fixed on a surface of concrete or asphalt, the supports must be fixed to a wall. This is easier if the trellis is erected in the corner where two walls join each other.

The plants may be set in the ground on either side of the trellis or grown in boxes or large pots if the ground has a hard surface.

As an alternative to trellis, a screen of rustic poles will be equally attractive; or it may be used to divide one part of the garden from another. Here, too, a rustic archway will add to the

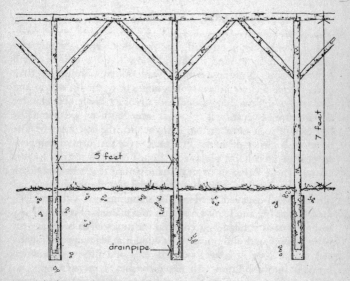

Erecting a Rustic Screen.

appearance of the garden, and over it the thornless Oregon blackberry or Japanese wineberry may be grown. When erecting rustic work remember that standing 6-7 ft. above ground and fully covered by climbing plants, it will have to support a considerable weight, especially when the plants are wet and during wind, so not only must the poles be strong and not too thin, but they must be inserted into the ground to a sufficient depth to enable them to take the weight without falling.

First, that part of the poles to be inserted below ground must be treated with creosote or some other wood preservative if it is to be long lasting. To make the poles as secure as possible, insert them into drain-pipes let into the ground to a depth of 2 ft. It is best to cement them in but otherwise pack soil tightly around the wall of the drain-pipes when in position. The screen may be given extra support if cross-pieces are fixed between the uprights and cross-bar whilst for a lower screen, the crosspieces may be fixed horizontally or diagonally and the plants trained accordingly.

PREPARATION OF THE SOIL

When planting against a wall, care must be taken in the preparation of the ground which must be supplied with moisture-holding humus. A brick wall will be more porous than one of stone and as the eaves of a house or outhouse will in any case tend to deprive the ground beneath of a considerable amount of moisture, especially if the wall faces south or west, and the bricks will soak up a certain amount too, the soil must be fortified with plenty of humus. This may take the form of dampened peat or used hops, obtainable from breweries usually for the asking. Those living in or near the towns of the industrial north will find cotton or wool shoddy a cheap and efficient type of humus. Well-decayed farmyard or stable manure will be ideal, for like shoddy and spent hops (and hop manure of a proprietary make is just as valuable), it contains the nitrogen so necessary for plant growth and will release it slowly for at least a year. Usually soil at the foot of a wall will be dry and lifeless and unless brought into condition will not grow heavy crops.

The soil must be prepared to a distance of at least 15 in. from the wall, for plants will send out their roots in search of food and moisture to at least this distance and to a similar depth. The best way is first to remove the soil to 15 in. in all directions and to place at the bottom several inches of humus, incorporating it also into the soil which was removed, at the same time adding an ounce of bone meal. For the plants to be hardy and productive, give the soil a dusting with a mixture of superphosphate and sulphate of potash when it is replaced. Allow the soil several days to consolidate before any planting is done.

Never plant too close to a drain, for the roots of plants will grow into it and may cause trouble. Neither is it desirable to plant too near the corner of a house where draughts may prove troublesome. It should be said that the garden soil of an industrial city may be sour, due to deposits of soot and sulphur over the years, and before mixing in the manures and fertilizers it should be dusted with hydrated lime, obtainable from a builder's merchant or garden shop. Lime will also make a heavy soil more friable. If wireworm is noticed, and they are the orange wire-like grubs of the click beatle, dust the ground with Lindex, for if unchecked, they will attack the roots of young plants, causing them to die back when otherwise they appear healthy.

Remember that fruit trees growing against a wall will occupy the same position for many years; some pears and peaches growing on the walls of old manor houses have been there for centuries and are still highly productive. This is because the soil was well prepared to begin with, whilst each year the plants are given a thick mulch of decayed manure to maintain the humus content of the soil and a balanced diet for the plants. This is all-important for the plants produce heavy crops which take a great deal of food and moisture from the soil each year and this must be put back.

Do not plant too close to a wall, especially in the case of fruit trees. Plant about 5–6 in. away which will allow the plants, especially the main stems, room to develop as they grow and permit the roots to obtain more moisture than if planted too close to the wall. Those fruit trees suitable for tub culture may be planted where there is 18 in. of soil over a cement base.

Permanent fruit trees may be planted at any time between 1 November and 1 March, whenever the soil is free from frost.

Plant firmly, spreading out the roots and treading the soil well as the roots are covered. Fruit trees should be planted about 9 in. deep to give them firm anchorage. Unless the soil is damp, water in the plants and tie in the main stem to the trellis or wall, or to a strong cane if the trellis is not yet in position.

A word should be said here about mulching. It is amazing how well plants will respond if given a mulch in June each year, by the formation of new wood upon which future crops will depend, and by the size and quality of the fruit. A dry soil will cause the fruits to fall long before they are mature, whilst they will stay small and lacking in juice if the plants do not receive sufficient moisture in summer. A thick mulch of decayed manure or composted straw, or a mixture of peat and used hops, will prevent moisture evaporation and reduce the need for artificial watering. This will keep the plants growing without check and enable the fruits to mature to their full flavour and size.

If manure in some form is not readily available, give the plants a thick dressing of peat and water occasionally with liquid manure, readily obtainable in proprietary make, or use a solution made from dried blood which is equally rich in nitrogen. Lawn mowings or decayed leaves may also be used in place of the peat, whilst old mushroom bed compost is ideal for this purpose if the garage or outhouse has been used to grow mushrooms.

Old-established wall plants (for those taking over an old property which may already have one or more fruit trees growing against a wall) will quickly respond after being given a mulch, by the formation of plenty of new wood so that much of the old may be removed in winter when the trees are pruned. Often, wall plants are neglected when once they have fulfilled their requirements in covering a bare wall, yet in order to bear a succession of heavy crops they must receive continuous care, pruning and feeding as well as spraying for pests and disease. Above all, never allow the plants to lack moisture at the roots in summer, whilst spraying the foliage in the evening during dry weather will freshen the plants and do much to keep away pests such as red spider which attack most wall plants where conditions are too dry.

Whenever heavy snow falls in winter, it should be shaken from the branches without delay and any broken branches must be cut back to the damaged part and the wound treated with tar. This will prevent 'bleeding' of plums and cherries and close up the wound so that disease and decay will not enter.

The French are the masters of growing fruits on walls, and in France almost every old wall produces its crop of Comice pears, using Glou Morceau as its pollinator. Both pears like to have their roots in moisture and their heads in the warm sunshine, when they will bear heavily, but they bloom and crop late and in England should be grown only in the south, preferably on a south or west wall.

Food Plants to Grow Against Walls

APRICOT

Whereas the peach grows better in the drier climate of eastern England, the apricot needs more moisture and grows better in the west, being successful as far north as Glasgow. It requires a soil with a high lime content and needs the shelter of a sunny wall on which it is grown, like the peach, as a fan-trained tree. The apricot is more difficult in that it suffers from die-back disease, which causes long-established shoots, for some unknown reason, to die right back. But on the other hand, apricots also fruit on the old and new wood if ripened by the sun of the preceding year so that when the old spurs have borne fruit for two seasons, they can be removed to make way for newly formed spurs.

Apricots must have sun to ripen the wood and so may be grown against the high wall of a lean-to greenhouse but the fan trees require a wall at least 18-20 ft. wide to develop, the stems being allowed to grow on as far as space permits, while the side shoots are pinched back in midsummer to about 1 in.

Though apricots are self-fertile, there will be a better set of fruit if the blossom is hand pollinated. This is essential where growing under glass. Dust the flowers with a camel-hair brush as they open when they are dry.

When the fruits have set and begin to swell, thin them to three per cluster and again to about 3 in. apart as they start to ripen. Allow the fruit to become fully ripe before picking and place them in a shallow tray lined with cotton wool.

For outdoors plant Hemskerk, the conical fruits being marked with red and, early to mature, are ready to eat by early August, and for later, Shipley's Blenheim bears small oval fruits of deepest orange and of rich flavour.

BLACKBERRIES AND HYBRID BERRIES

For a bleak north wall or to cover a trellis which has been erected to hide a dustbin or outhouse, there is no better plant than the blackberry or its numerous hybrids. In winter, the leaves usually take on rich crimson colours, later turning golden yellow before they fall. In addition, the young leaves have the beauty of ferns as they unfold in spring. The fruits are ready to use in late summer and in autumn when they may be used for jams and jellies or in pies and flans, whilst they freeze better than any fruits, never becoming 'mushy'.

They require a soil containing plenty of humus, so work in whatever materials are available. Used hops or old manure are ideal for they need these fertilizers to hold moisture, otherwise the fruit will be hard and seedy and completely lacking in juice. In a dry summer, give a mulch of lawn mowings or peat and keep the plants supplied with moisture.

Plant in November 3 in. deep and about 8ft. apart and they will soon cover a trellis to this height and width. Newly planted canes are cut back to within 6 in. of soil level. As the fruit is borne on the new and old wood, the shoots are merely tied in so as to hide the trellis and there is little need for pruning except for the removal of dead wood. In April each year, give each plant a quarter of an ounce of sulphate of potash and rake into the soil.

VARIETIES OF BLACKBERRY

Bedford Giant. It is one of the best for canning and freezing and is one of the earliest, ripening its fruit early in August. It is large, sweet and juicy but in some years does not crop as heavily as Himalaya Giant.

Himalaya Giant. Raised from seed brought into Europe from the Himalayas, it is a hardy and vigorous grower and as it bears as heavily on the old wood as on the new, it produces a huge crop. It will provide a windbreak or impenetrable hedge trained along wires. The fruit is ready late in August.

John Innes. Raised in the 1920s by Sir Daniel Hall, it crops well on the old canes and bears a large sweet berry during October, but in the north it is too late unless given a sunny position. The canes grow to 8 ft.

King's Acre Berry. Ripening its fruit mid-August, the blackish-red fruits part from the cane like raspberries thus making it excellent for dessert and jams, but it does not freeze so well.

Oregon Thornless. With its handsome divided foliage, it is as ornamental as it is useful. Making canes 6-8 ft. long, it bears its fruit in large clusters, a fully grown plant bearing up to ten pounds, and, as its name implies, it is thornless.

VARIETIES OF HYBRID BERRIES

They have the blackberry for a parent and are mostly derived from a cross with the loganberry, itself a hybrid berry.

Boysenberry. Making canes up to 8 ft. long, it bears a heavy crop of dark red fruits in August with a distinct sharp and pleasant flavour.

Japanese Wineberry. A handsome plant, the 6 ft. thornless stems being covered in soft crimson hairs whilst the small amber-coloured fruit is sharp and refreshing to the taste. It is the first of the hybrid berries, ready mid-July.

Loganberry. The best strain is LY59, vigorous growing, making canes 8 ft. long, but they tend to be brittle and break easily, so should not be grown in a windswept garden. Whilst immune to frost, it does not like cold winds. There is a thornless variety bearing a long tapering fruit which retains its core and bottles and freezes well. The dull red fruits ripen in August. The loganberry bears its fruit only on the new wood and after fruiting, the canes are cut back to within 3 in. of soil level and the new season's canes tied in.

Lowberry. Like most hybrid berries, of American origin, bearing a jet-black fruit which is 1 in. long and which does not part from its core, bottling well. It has the sweetness and flavour of the blackberry.

Youngberry. The canes grow to 6 ft., the purple-black fruits maturing early August. They are often of 1 in. diameter and sweet and juicy, yielding up to ten pounds from a single plant. Like the loganberry, it crops better in warmer districts.

CHERRY (MORELLO)

Because they are difficult to pollinate and take several years to bear a reasonable crop, sweet cherries are not suitable for wall planting in preference to any of the other fruits. For a north wall, however, where little else will grow, the Morello cherries used for cooking may be planted. If there is room, plant two varieties, Kentish Red which is ripe by the end of July, and the Morello itself, which ripens a month later and will pollinate the other. These are the acid or sour cherries and are excellent for bottling to use in winter for tarts and flans. If they have a fault it is that they are occasionally troubled by Brown Rot so that any diseased wood must be removed as soon as it is observed.

Morello cherries bear their fruit on the previous season's wood, so the aim must be to encourage a continual supply of new wood. The trees are grown in fan formation and all lateral shoots are cut back halfway in autumn. In spring the side shoots are pinched back to within 2 in. of the new season's growth.

On the previous year's shoots will be found the blossom buds and it is upon these that the present year's fruit is borne. Several buds will be seen, but only one is retained and this will continue to grow through summer for fruiting next season. Like sweet cherries (and plums too), Morellos can be allowed to carry plenty of wood without any reduction in the amount of fruit but if the trees make too much growth, root pruning may be done in winter as for plums.

Whether Morellos are a better crop than blackberries for a northerly wall is doubtful but there may be room for blackberries elsewhere.

CUCUMBER

There is a Chinese climbing variety sufficiently hardy to grow outdoors in the British Isles and if given a sunny wall or trellis, it will bear heavily until cut down by early winter frosts. The smooth skinned fruit grows 18 in. long and $1\frac{1}{2}$ in. thick and will retain its quality for several weeks after removal from the plant.

Seed is sown in small pots containing John Innes compost, obtainable from garden shops, sowing in March in the sunny window of a warm room and setting out the plants about 1 June. Plant in deep boxes containing a compost of fresh loam and decayed manure, spacing the plants 2 ft. apart. As the plants continue to grow, lateral shoots are stopped at the second leaf so that the plants do not make too much foliage. During warm, dry weather water copiously and once each week feed with dilute manure water when the first fruits begin to form. It will also be advisable to spray the foliage daily to prevent red spider and to help the flowers to set, but pollination by hand is not necessary.

FIGS

Fig plants decorate the walls of many basement courtyards in Georgian Bath where grows the best of all outdoor varieties, the suitably named Brunswick, so called after the royal house of that name, the large pale green fruits having sweet white flesh. Along the western side of Britain and especially in sight of the sea, figs will flourish in all but the most exposed gardens; but on the eastern side, they grow well outdoors only as far north as the Wash. Here may be planted the hardier Black Ischia which produces its purple-black fruits with crimson flesh in profusion. Brown Turkey is also excellent and does as well outdoors as inside.

In an average year, outdoor figs will ripen to perfection and there is no more delicious fruit to have as dessert, accompanied by a mellow Madeira wine.

Figs are ideal plants to cover the walls of a town courtyard for they crop better where the roots are restricted by planting in soil which is surrounded on all sides by stones or cement, or plant directly over a base made compact by ramming. This will prevent the plant forming a tap root. Or again, remove soil to a depth of 18 ins. and after putting in a brick base, pour over it 1 in. of cement and allow it to set hard. Then replace the soil, mixing in some lime rubble but no manure, for rank soil will cause the plant to make excess foliage at the expense of fruit and in poor soil figs make plenty of leaf. Where none of this is practical, then plant in the pots in which the figs were raised.

Plant in March, making the soil compact about the roots and always pot-grow plants. Through summer, water copiously; a mulch of decayed garden compost given in June will help retain moisture in the soil.

Figs seem to bear well in the horizontal form and as the fruit is produced on the new season's wood, the only pruning given to established trees is to limit the shoots produced from each fruit bud. Late in July, the replacement shoot is stopped at the fourth leaf. Cutting back too early will upset the balance of the plant for the fruit expected to mature the following summer will form too quickly, at the expense of wood. Yet if the shoot is not pinched back, the fruit will not develop and will turn yellow and fall.

The fruits form at the leaf axils where the leaves join the stem, where they remain until the following summer. In spring they will begin to swell and continue to do so until late August. They are gathered just as they begin to split, not before. Place them in trays lined with cotton wool and in a cool, frost-free room they will keep for several weeks until reaching perfection.

If unrestricted, plants will eventually get right out of hand and make excessive growth; they will then have to be root pruned or will continue to make leaf and little fruit.

Soil is removed to a distance of about 3 ft. from the main stem and to a depth of 18 in., the large roots are cut back to 2 ft. from the plant but not the smaller fibrous roots. Replace the soil, ramming it well down.

Figs are propagated from suckers which form around the main stem. They should be detached with their roots and grown on in pots for twelve months.

Figs are rarely troubled by pests or disease. They are of easy culture and the only cause of disappointment is when hard frosts kill the young shoots. In a severe winter, drape some old muslin or plastic sheeting from the top of the wall over the plant and remove this towards the end of February. Usually, however, a fig will receive all the protection necessary from a warm wall.

GOOSEBERRY

Gooseberries prefer cool conditions, hence most varieties grow better in the north and midlands. They are more tolerant of frost and cold winds than any fruits with the exception of blackberries, and they require a light, well-drained soil containing humus in the form of peat or decayed manure, or used hops. Too much nitrogen should be avoided as this will encourage outbreaks of mildew. The plants are best grown 'hard' (when the plants do not make too much soft growth) and for this purpose, give each a one ounce dressing of sulphate of potash in spring. Planting is done in November or at any time in winter when the soil is not frozen. Gooseberries grow on a leg and in this way differ from blackcurrants which form suckers, hence they may be grown as cordons or double cordons against a trellis where they will grow to a height of 4 ft. A position of semi-shade will suit them well, but mulch in June to conserve moisture in the soil.

The single cordon is made by cutting back all lateral shoots to a single bud, the leader or extension shoot being grown on. All new growth formed in summer is pinched back to within 2 in. of the base or stem in late July after fruiting.

A double cordon is formed by cutting back the main stem to two buds about 9 in. above ground, the newly formed shoots being trained (on canes), first at an angle of 45°, then horizontally. Later, cut back to two upward buds, one on either side of the stem, and grow on the shoots in an upward direction to the required height. The best varieties to grow as cordons are those of upright habit such as the white fruiting Langley Gage, the green Gunner, Whitesmith or Bedford Red. Broom Girl and Bedford Yellow are also excellent yellow dessert varieties.

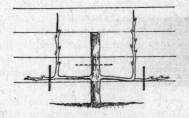

Forming a double cordon.

NECTARINE

It is a smooth-skinned 'peach', or a peach without its 'bloom' and enjoys the same climatic conditions and culture, i.e. a soil containing plenty of lime rubble and a position where the summer sunshine can ripen its wood, and its fruit. Prune exactly as for peaches (see p. 00) and in spring, give a liberal mulching of decayed manure. Also, whilst the fruit is swelling, give ample supplies of water. If lacking moisture, the fruit will fall early, though watering must cease when once the fruit starts to ripen.

Early Rivers is the best for outdoors, cropping heavily, its brilliant red fruits maturing early in August. For later, Lord Napier, with pale green fruits flushed with red; and Humboldt, its medium-size fruits of deepest orange being ripe by early September.

PEACH

Though they are native to Central China, perhaps it may not be realized that in England peaches may be grown in the open without any means of protection, against a sunny wall as far north as a line drawn from Chester to the Wash and in East Anglia and Kent. This is the climate, hot and dry in summer, cold in winter, that suits it best. Farther north, it may be grown on the sunny back wall of a lean-to greenhouse.

It is the most beautiful of trees when in blossom; the flowers appear at least two weeks before the leaves and last for four weeks.

Like all stone fruits, peaches enjoy a soil containing plenty of lime, but unlike plums, they require almost no nitrogenous manure. All that is necessary is to work into the soil at planting time, which is November, two ounces of bone meal for each plant and at the same time, give a light dressing of lime. The soil must be kept moist in summer, a mulch early in June helping in this respect. Peaches are self-fertile and set heavy crops with their own pollen, but if the weather is cold when the blossom appears, hand pollinate, using a camel-hair brush.

Like plums, peaches crop best as fan-trained trees but as they bear fruit on the new season's wood, this must be continually encouraged to form. In March, new growth is cut back by about a third whilst the tips of the side growths are pinched out in mid-summer when about 2 in. long. At the base of these shoots appears a single wood-bud to grow-on. On this wood will be borne next year's fruit and the shoot which has borne this year's fruit is removed. However, in the early years, pruning is on the same lines as the renewal system for apples; that is, whilst the tree is being built up, the shoots which have borne fuit are allowed to

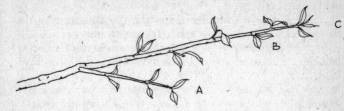

Pruning a Peach.

A · Replacement shoot to tie in.
B · Side growths pinched back.
C · Leader growing away.

grow on until about 18 in. long. These are then fastened to the wall and the tips pinched back to a wood bud. It is on the wood of this bud that next year's fruit is borne. The wood buds are small and pointed, while the blossom buds are round and fat. All shoots next to a leaf should be pinched back above the second leaf.

If there is space for two varieties, plant Hale's Early or Peregrine, both being hardy and reliable, with fruit ready early in August; and for late September either Barrington or Royal George, both bearing large, well-coloured fruits of delicious flavour.

Peaches need at least 18 ft. in width and in height where growing against a wall and to restrict growth, root prune as for plums. (see p. 00).

In most years it will be necessary to thin the fruit but this is not done until after 'stoning'. This is a natural falling off of fruits when about walnut size. About 6 in. should be allowed between each fruit.

The fruit is ripe if it feels just soft when gently pressed at the base, and is removed by placing the palm of the hand beneath it and moving it in an upwards direction, when it will part from its stem. The fruits are placed in shallow trays lined with cotton wool.

PESTS AND DISEASES

Leaf Curl. It attacks the leaves and also the stems, causing the leaves to curl up at the edges and to fall prematurely. The disease winters on the wood, so early in February spray with Orthocide or a copper fungicide and repeat in autumn after the leaves have fallen.

Mealy Bug. It sometimes occurs on the peach as on vines, and is a small beetle which produces a mass of cotton wool-like excreta. To prevent an attack, spray with winter wash in late December.

PEARS

Apples are of European, pears of Asiatic origin, and enjoy the warmth of the east to grow and mature. In consequence, choice of variety is important, the later maturing varieties such as Comice and Glou Morceau being grown south of the Thames or along the Severn Valley from Gloucester to Worcester and Hereford. North of the Thames the three most reliable pears are Conference, Laxton's Superb and Dr Jules Guyot, for each blooms late and so, in most seasons, misses the frosts.

Pears are usually grown in the espalier or horizontal form and a pear tree trained in this way will cover a wall very quickly, yet it has a very long life and in addition to its fruit, there will be the

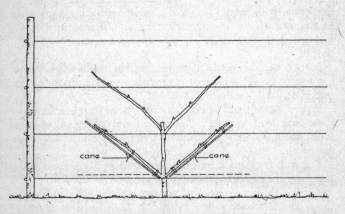

Training a pear to the horizontal form (espalier)

charming greyish-white blossom in early summer and the rich colours of its foliage in autumn. Remember, though, that espaliers require at least 12 ft. to form their arms.

Pears require plenty of humus to make their rapid growth and as nitrogen is important, give the trees a one ounce dressing of sulphate of ammonia in spring each year and a mulch of decayed manure in July. When planting, keep the scion of the rootstock onto which the variety was grafted above soil level, otherwise it will form roots at the graft.

To train a maiden or one-year-old tree, shorten the stem in spring to 18 in. above soil level, to a point where there are two buds, one facing right, the other left. The laterals which form from these buds are tied to strong wires stretched across the wall, the extension or leader shoot being allowed to grow on unchecked until it is again cut back to two more buds about 15 in. above the first two. In this way a new tier is formed each year and to encourage fruiting spurs, all shoots along the arms are pruned back in summer to within 5-6 in. of the main stem or arm.

As the side arms continue to make growth, this is shortened back to half of the newly formed wood in winter, cutting back to a bud which is to form the extension shoot.

If the side buds show a tendency to make their growth in an upward direction, the wood should be tied to canes which in turn are tied in to the wires at an angle of 45° at first, being gradually reduced to the horizontal form.

Pears and also apples may be grown as cordons, planting them against a framework of trellis or galvanized wires to which the plants are fastened. Maiden trees are planted at an oblique angle rather than upright and spaced 3 ft. apart. The main stem is not pruned and in the first year pruning consists of cutting back the lateral shoots in August to 6 in. from the main stem. This will ensure the formation of fruiting spurs. Not until the tree has reached its required height, which will be as much as 20ft. if growing against the end wall of a large house, is the leader stopped so that the tree can concentrate on forming fruit rather than on making new growth. It will form one tier every year.

Trees in cordon form also crop heavily as their growth is restricted and close planting is a help to pollination. However, excessive pruning of pears should be avoided as this encourages too much soft growth and makes the trees liable to scab, the most troublesome of pear diseases.

Pears must be harvested in exactly the right condition, when neither too hard nor too soft. This can be determined by lifting one of the fruits in the palm of the hand; if it parts from the tree it is ripe. Most early varieties must be eaten from the tree but late varieties will store for several months in an airy room, though they require more warmth than apples or they will sweat. They are the prima donnas of the world of fruit, a Mozart minuet compared with the fullness of a Beethoven symphony to which Cox's Orange apples may be likened, and they need a temperature of 45°-48° F. to store in peak condition. Remove them from the tree with care, using a gentle lift with the palm rather than with the fingers so as not to bruise them, and place upright in a wooden seed tray lined with cotton wool. They should not touch each other.

PESTS AND DISEASES

Brown Rot Blossom Wilt. The fungus attacks apples, pears and cherries, causing the blossom to turn brown and die. It may also attack the stems causing them to die back. For pears and apples, spray with petroleum-oil wash in January.

Leaf Scorch. Similar to leaf curl of peaches, it causes the leaves to turn brown and curl up at the edges whilst the fruits will be small and hard. It may be caused by potash deficiency, so if observed give each tree a two ounce dressing of muriate of potash.

Midge. The pest, which is a tiny grey midge, lays in the blossom as it opens, the white maggots later eating into the fruits making them unusable. Those fruits which fall ensure that the grubs winter underground to pupate as midges in spring. As routine, dust the trees with derris as soon as the blossom opens.

POLLINATION

As with apples and plums, pears should have a pollinator to set heavy crops and which will be in bloom together. Even so, Conference will not pollinate Beurré d'Amanlis neither will Seckle pollinate Louise Bonne. Plant together (and two trees are better than one) those which bloom early: Beurré Hardy, Conférence, Louise Bonne, Durondeau.

Those which bloom mid-season: Beurré Bedford, Glou Morceau, Thompson's, William's Bon Cretien.

Those which bloom late: Dr Jules Guyot, Doyenne du Comice, Fertility, Laxton's Superb, Winter Nelis.

VARIETIES WHICH MATURE JULY-SEPTEMBER

Beurré Hardy. It is hardy and suitable for a northern garden, maturing late September, and it bears heavily. The fruit has pleasant rose-tinted flesh and a delicate rose perfume.

Dr Jules Guyot. A good cordon tree, it is fertile and hardy, the pale golden fruit having the musky flavour of William's pear. Valuable in that it blooms late and misses the frosts. It is the best pollinator for late pears.

Jargonelle. Another hardy variety which does as well in the north as in the warmer parts and so may be grown against a north wall. It is also highly resistant to scab. The small green and brown tapering fruit is of delicate flavour. But it is a triploid, requiring two pollinators which bloom early for it is unable to pollinate in return. Durondeau and William's are the best.

Laxton's Foremost. A William's seedling and a splendid late September pear which crops well on a west wall. The handsome fruit has a pale golden skin and buttery flesh, being in no way 'gritty'.

William's Bon Cretien. Of upright habit, it makes an excellent cordon and bears heavy crops of pale yellow fruit, full of juice and flavour. Use Dr Guyot or Conference as pollinators. It is the Bartlett pear of the American canners.

VARIETIES WHICH MATURE IN OCTOBER AND NOVEMBER

These pears should be confined to gardens in the south, for in the north they do not ripen fully.

Bergamotte d'Esperen. Raised a century ago by a Major Esperen, it ripens well only on a sunny wall, when the pale yellow fruit remains sweet and juicy until March if carefully stored.

Bristol Cross. Raised at Long Ashton, it crops well in the moist climate of the West Country, yielding consistently heavy crops of yellow, russetted fruits which are sweet and juicy.

Conference. Hardy, fertile and long keeping, it is probably the best all-round pear ever introduced, the long tapering pale green fruits being sweet and juicy. It does not crop well in an exposed garden.

Doyenne du Comice. With its melting cinnamon-flavoured flesh, it is the best of all pears, but crops well only if its roots are in a rich humus-laden soil and its head in warm sunshine so should not be grown far north of the Thames. It is pollinated by Bristol Cross or Glou Morceau.

Durondeau. A very good pear for November eating, the long tapering fruit having a coppery-red skin and being sweet and juicy. It is also a good pollinator.

Glou Morceau. Of compact, upright growth it requires a warm wall to crop well, its small green fruits having a muscatel flavour and being free from 'grit'. Like Comice, it is at its best in December.

Packham's Triumph. Introduced from New Zealand, it is an 'easy Comice', cropping more heavily than Comice in Britain. If harvested in late October, it will keep until the new year.

Thompson's. One of the easiest and best late pears, cropping well and being at its best just before Christmas when it should be enjoyed with a mature port before bed-time.

PLUMS AND GAGES
As plums are the first of the fruits to bloom, they are more susceptible to frost then other fruits, yet no fruit, not even the peach or pear, possesses quite the flavour of a choice dessert plum, eaten from the tree warm with the late summer sunshine and nowhere do they grow better than against a warm wall though they ripen in less sunlight than pears. On a wall they should be grown in the fan-shaped form and in this way the most economic use of the walls will be made. In a soil well supplied with nitrogen the trees will reach a height of 10 ft. and the same across, so if there is room for more than one they should be planted at least 12 ft. apart. Plums thrive on nitrogenous manures and frequent mulchings during summer for they are by nature moisture-loving plants. Decayed farmyard manure is ideal but if this is difficult to obtain, use for a mulch garden compost or peat and in spring each year, give each tree a one ounce dressing of sulphate of ammonia.

Plums do better on a westerly wall, where they receive the late afternoon sun. They will come quickly into bearing and require the minimum of pruning since they form their fruit buds along the whole length of the stems. Pruning is best done in spring when the buds are beginning to burst. At this time the wounds heal quickly and there is no 'bleeding' which is a source of trouble to all stone fruits, allowing entrance to the dreaded silver leaf disease which derives its nourishment from the tree cells. Do not prune plums in winter.

If a tree is making too much growth, it should be root pruned every fourth year. It is necessary to remove the soil to expose the roots growing away from the wall to a distance of 3 ft. Then the longer roots are cut back with the pruners, leaving untouched the fibrous roots nearer the stem. This will reduce the vigour of the tree. The soil is then trodden back and the tree mulched.

To form a fan-shaped tree, a maiden is cut back to upward buds, one on either side of the stem and about 12 in. above the scion. These will 'break' to form the first pair of arms. After a season's growth, they are cut back to two buds 18 in. above the fork, and from these the fan-trained tree is trained. In spring, each shoot is cut back to two more buds and so on until the tree is formed. Pruning then consists of pinching back about a third of the new wood and all side shoots early in May, but when the tree has been shaped very little pruning is required.

POLLINATION

Plums may be grown anywhere in Britain and expected to ripen their fruit, though as they flower earlier than other tree fruits, they are more susceptible to frost damage. Against this it may be said that the self-fertile varieties will set heavy crops with their own pollen so that if Victoria plums are most enjoyed several plants of this variety may be grown together, to the exclusion of all others. The following plums are self-fertile; they need no pollinator but will set even heavier crops with one:

Belle de Louvain	(Early)
Denniston's Superb	(Early)
Early Transparent Gage	(Early)
Laxton's Gage	(Late)
Monarch	(Early)

| Oullin's Golden Gage | (Late) |
| Victoria | (Mid-season) |

They will pollinate most of the self-sterile varieties as are the following:

Bryanston Gage	(Mid-season)
Coe's Golden Drop	(Early)
Count Althan's Gage	(Early)
Greengage	(Mid-season)
Kirke's Blue	(Mid-season)
Late Transparent Gage	(Late)
Laxton's Delicious	(Late)
Pond's Seedling	(Late)
Severn Cross	(Early)
Thames Cross	(Early)

Although Coe's Golden and Count Althan's Gage are self-sterile, they will pollinate each other and are unsurpassable for flavour, but usually it is advisable to plant a self-fertile variety with one that is self-sterile and in bloom at the same time.

PESTS AND DISEASES

Aphis. It may be troublesome for plants growing against a wall, the greenfly clustering on the underside of the leaves, sucking the sap and causing the leaves to turn brown and curl up. Eggs are laid on the branches in late autumn and hatch out in spring. Spray with a tar-oil wash in December which will kill the eggs.

Brown Rot. It is most destructive as the brown fungus attacks through the leaves causing them to curl and die, and from there it attacks the fruiting spurs also causing them to die back.

The same disease also attacks the blossom when it is known as blossom wilt, causing the blossom to die before it has set fruit. To control, spray with petroleum oil in January and with one per cent lime-sulphur just before the blossom opens. This will also destroy the eggs of aphis and keep red spider under control.

Sawfly. The eggs are laid in the flowers where the grubs remain until the fruits begin to form when they tunnel inside making the fruits unfit to use. At petal fall, spray with Lindex (one ounce to two gallons of water).

Silver Leaf. The most destructive of all plum diseases, the leaves taking on a silver appearance. Later it attacks the wood, causing it to decay. The fungus can live on dead wood which must be removed and destroyed between April and 1 July (by Government order). During summer, where any cuts have been made on the branches, plums exude a gummy substance which will heal up a wound. If broken branches occur in winter, treat the wound with white lead paint to prevent the disease entering.

PLUMS AND GAGES WHICH RIPEN IN AUGUST

Belle de Louvain. A valuable dual-purpose plum, the large purple fruits eating well from the tree, whilst they are sweet and of excellent flavour when stewed. Valuable for a frosty garden as it blooms late.

Denniston's Superb. A plum-gage cross, its green fruit flushed with crimson having the true greengage flavour. Raised in New York in 1835, it is hardy, sets a heavy crop with its own pollen and (with Victoria) acts as a pollinator for more plums than any other variety.

Early Transparent Gage. A superb variety, setting a heavy crop with its own pollen, but it blooms early and may be caught by frost. The pale apricot skin shows the stone through it and when ripe it has the distinct apricot fragrance.

Oullin's Golden Gage. A plum-greengage cross with Denniston's, it remains one of the best ever raised, the large golden fruits being sweet and juicy and they bottle well. It blooms late and usually misses the frosts.

Victoria. The finest plum ever introduced and named in honour of a great queen and mother. The large red oval fruits are delicious when ripe and bottle well. If it has a fault, it is that its brittle wood too easily breaks.

PLUMS AND GAGES WHICH RIPEN IN SEPTEMBER

Angelina Burdett. Old Thomas Hogg, who had his nursery where now is Paddington Station, said that when ripe 'it forms a perfect sweetmeat' as indeed it does. The purple fruit is speckled brown. It will remain in condition for nearly a month after harvesting.

Bryanston Gage. It needs Victoria as a pollinator, when it crops profusely, its pale green fruits being speckled with crimson.

Count Althan's Gage. An outstanding plum-gage, the round crimson-purple fruits having the true gage flavour whilst it bottles well. It is pollinated by Oullin's or Thames Cross.

Greengage. In my Somerset orchard, where it grew in a rich deep loam, it collapsed one year with the weight of fruit it grew, the greenish-yellow gages being sweet and melting. It also does well on chalk.

Pond's Seedling. Not especially good for dessert but it bottles well and blooms late so usually misses the frosts. It also crops well in a dry chalk soil. The rose-red fruit is large and handsome.

Thames Cross. Pollinates Count Althan's and vice versa. It is a large oval golden plum, delicious from the tree (it has Coe's Golden as a parent) and bottles well.

PLUMS AND GAGES WHICH RIPEN IN OCTOBER

Coe's Golden Drop. One of the most delicious of all plums, raised two hundred years ago by Gervaise Coe, gardener at Hengrave Hall, its amber yellow skin and flesh resembling an apricot in its eating.

Laxton's Delicious. It has Coe's Golden Drop for a parent but crops more heavily, whilst it will keep for a fortnight after picking in late October. It blooms late so misses the frosts and is pollinated by Oullin's Gage. It is yellow when ripe, flushed with red.

RUNNER AND CLIMBING BEANS

To clothe a wall or trellis in summer, the climbing beans will prove colourful with their bright scarlet flowers and will provide heavy crops of tender green beans from early August until mid-October. What is more, they may be frozen or preserved by salting, to enjoy during winter when vegetables are expensive.

Plants may be grown in deep boxes and trained up canes or stakes (laths) fastened to wires fixed 2 in. from a wall; or even up strong twine. Or they may be grown against wire netting or a trellis, either fixed to a wall or used to hide an unsightly corner. The plants require full sunlight to be a success and a rich soil, in which plenty of decayed manure is incorporated, together with one ounce of superphosphate of lime and sulphate of potash (mixed together) per square yard of soil.

Seed is sown singly 1 in. deep and 6 in. apart in early May, not before, as climbing beans are tender and may be caught by frost. The plants should not appear above the soil until late May. As soon as growth is seen, put the stakes in position close to the beans; they should be at least 6 ft. high for the plants can reach up to 8 ft. within two months. Alternatively, as beans transplant well, seed may be sown in 2 in. deep boxes in a sunny window early in May and the plants set out when 2 in. tall at the end of the month.

Water the plants copiously throughout summer and when the first beans begin to form, give an occasional watering with diluted liquid manure which is obtainable in bottles of proprietary make from garden shops and is clean to use. This will make for tender beans and increase the yield. The plants will also benefit from a daily syringe or spraying with clean water during dry weather. This will prevent an outbreak of red spider and help to pollinate the flowers. It will also keep the beans fresh and succulent.

There are a number of climbing beans which differ from scarlet runners. One is the Blue Coco bean, the large leaves and stems being of a bright purple colour whilst the long beans are of similar colouring with a distinctive flavour. The beans, which are borne in clusters at regular intervals, should be steamed with a little butter or margarine rather than boiled in order to bring out the subtle flavour.

The Blue Lake bean, of American origin, is equally delicious. It is really a climbing French bean with white flowers and bears small, round stringless pods of bluish-green which are quick to mature and delicious when cooked. Another climbing French bean is Tender and True, also known as the Guernsey Runner for it is grown on the island in place of the scarlet runner. It crops from top to bottom of the stems but it does well only in the warmer parts of Britain. Hardier and similar is Kentucky Wonder; also Sutton's new bean, Amateur's Pride, which has the mild flavour of dwarf beans.

Of scarlet runners, Crusader is outstanding; it bears heavy crops of long, fleshy pods and in dry weather does not drop its buds. Streamline bears long, narrow stringless beans and Yardstick combines length and straightness of pod with superb quality.

To preserve beans, pick when quite young, top and tail and remove the string before slicing into a wide-top glass or earthenware jar. To every 2 in. depth of beans, add a half-inch layer of salt and continue until the jar is filled. Cover the top of the jar and keep in a dark place when they will remain fresh for a year or more.

STRAWBERRIES

Herr Hummel's amazing remontant, Sojana, introduced into Britain in 1957, has given satisfaction. It forms long runners and can therefore be grown against a wall or trellis upon which it will grow to 6 ft. or more in height, or it may be grown along the ground like a rambler rose and covered with continuous cloches. It may also be grown in pots and trained up long canes arranged fan-wise. It should be given shelter from cold winds, and as it crops from early August until late November it requires a well-nourished soil and must never lack moisture. If it is grown in pots, insert them in the ground to half the height of the pots to prevent them from being blown over and to conserve moisture. A sunny position is also essential for it to bear well in autumn. It also requires a permanent position for it is a perennial, dying back in winter to come into growth again in spring when the soil should receive a liberal dressing with decayed manure. Set out the plants 3 ft. apart in late autumn.

As much as fourteen pounds of fruit may be obtained in one season from a single plant and its runners if it is fed well and kept moist at the roots. The fruit is bright red with the flavour of alpine strawberries and hangs in trusses of three or four. It is produced all the way up the stems. Where plants are grown upright, regular attention to tying is important. There is no tedious weeding, no disbudding, no strawing to keep the fruit clean, no trouble from slugs, and its upright habit makes it possible to produce strawberries in a restricted area, or even where there is no garden at all.

VINES

Delicious grapes may be obtained from a wall which has a south or west aspect. The vine is hardier than the fig and if it receives sufficient sun to ripen the fruit, can be grown anywhere. The world's largest vine is in Stirlingshire.

Vines may be grown against a pole as cordons entirely in the open, like rambler roses, but they will give better results grown in the horizontal form against a wall or trellis, or trained to strong galvanized wires. They require much the same treatment as espalier pears.

Plant from pots in autumn against a wall or where there is a lean-to available, plant the roots outside the greenhouse at one end and take the canes in through a hole made by the removal of a brick or sheet of glass and train over the back wall, which it will soon cover.

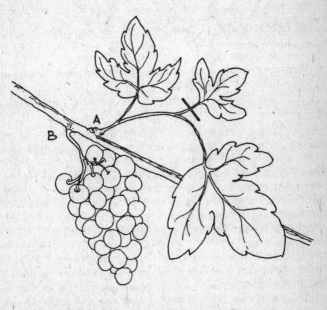

A : Foliage Bud   B : Fruit Bud

During winter, the cane is cut back to the three lowest buds about 15 in. from soil level, the cut being made immediately above a bud growing in an upward direction. This will form the leader shoot and shoots from the two other buds are trained one on either side, first in an upright direction, then when growth becomes vigorous, tie in the shoots to wires in a horizontal position. At the end of summer the leader shoot is cut back again to three buds about 15 in. above the first two arms, and so on until the wall is covered, one pair of arms being formed each year; they will reach 10 ft. or more in each direction. At the end of summer when the leader shoot is pruned these are also cut back to about half their growth, and on these rods grapes will be borne next year. Every eye, in fact, may develop a shoot which will be capable of bearing a bunch or two of grapes. Alternatively, the weaker arm may be cut to two eyes at the base.

A vine, however well grown, cannot be expected to bear fruit in plenty on both the new and old wood so one has the choice of:

(a) Allowing one or two new rods to make considerable growth and restricting all other new growth. This is known as the long rod system.

(b) Allowing the plant to bear a large number of growths, but keeping them shortened back.

(c) Cutting back all new wood to the main stem to form the spur system.

Apart from cutting back extension shoots at the end of summer, all pruning of vines is done in winter, during the dormant period before the sap begins to rise. New Year's Day is usually chosen by specialists to begin pruning which should be completed by the end of the month. With the long rod system (a), the remaining rod (where one has been cut back) is tied in, for on it will be borne next year's crop, and that from the stronger of the two base buds is grown on to provide the following year's crop.

To prevent overcrowding, all laterals are cut back to two buds, one of which will bear the fruit and the other the leaves which provide the plant with its nourishment.

The spur system (c) is that by which one rod is allowed to grow on during the first year and alternate buds are selected on each side of the stem to produce short laterals the following season. These will bear fruit and are stopped at the first joint after the bunch has formed. The shoots are cut back to two buds in winter from which the fruit and leaf growths are formed the following year; and so on. This will build up a system of spurs similar to that of apples and pears grown as espaliers or cordons.

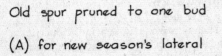

Old spur pruned to one bud

(A) for new season's lateral

The pinching of laterals in summer is done over a period of a week or more so as not to check the growing plant. Later, all lateral growths formed from the non-fruiting lateral are pinched back when they have formed one leaf so that the energies of the plant are concentrated into forming fruit.

When planting a vine, prepare a hole at least 18 in. deep and at the bottom, as for figs, ram hard down a 6 in. layer of brick or mortar. Into the soil, mix some decayed manure and a sprinkling or bone meal and sulphate of potash. Plant firmly and space the vines at least 10 ft. apart.

For outdoors, plant Royal Muscadine, Muscat de Sauner, or Golden Queen which bear large golden yellow grapes. Others of excellence are Buckland Sweetwater and Angevine Oberlin, the latter almost white. In blacks, Hâtif Noir de Marseilles does well in the open and under glass, but Black Hamburgh is supreme.

Earlier crops may be enjoyed where there is a cold greenhouse, and earlier still where some degree of warmth is available. A winter temperature of 40°-42°F. (5°-6°C.) is all that is necessary and this may rise in spring to 58°-60°F. (14°-15°C.) when the flowers appear. Under glass, the flowers are protected from late frosts. In spring a moist atmosphere created by frequent syringing will encourage the buds to break, and this should be maintained until the fruit has set.

Where there is overcrowding of the bunches, the grapes should be thinned. The plants require copious watering in summer to help the fruits to swell. They will be ready to remove (with scissors) when nicely coloured and of good size although certain varieties, like Prècose de Malingre, a golden yellow grape, remain quite small.

The old Strawberry vine is worth a mention here. It grows along the south coast and the Severn Valley, usually planted against a porch over which its bunches of rosy-red grapes hang in large bunches; they really do taste like strawberries whilst the plant, with its pale green leaves, is most attractive. But for its first two years do not let it bear more than two or three bunches.

It should be planted from pots which is done in October and it is advisable to cover the roots with straw and sacking during the cold December–February period for it is not quite hardy.

PESTS AND DISEASES

Mealy Bug. It attacks peaches too but with vines, lives under the paper-like bark which should be scraped regularly and painted with methylated spirit afterwards.

Mildew. It attacks the leaves in a wet, humid year as a grey powder causing them to fall and, if unchecked, will appear on the grapes. To prevent, dust the foliage in May and in July with flowers of sulphur.

Vine Weevil. The larva is creamy-white and hides in the soil by day, attacking the stems at night. There should be no trouble if the soil around the plant is soaked with Lindex solution in early spring and again about midsummer.

CHAPTER THREE

FOOD FROM A WINDOW-BOX, SINK OR TROUGH

Dwarf compact lettuces, radishes, and the small growing herbs, as well as trailing nasturtiums and ground ivy to drape over the sides, may all be grown in a window-box with complete success. Parsley, the richest source of vitamin A in all the vegetable kingdom and also rich in iron, does well given window-box culture, as do primroses, whose flowers and fresh crinkled leaves may be used in a spring salad before they become too large and tough. French beans do well in a deep window-box and Tiny Tim tomato crops admirably. Eat its tomatoes of the size of marbles, just as they are or have them with scrambled eggs or cheese, for the skins are thin and the fruits are sweet and juicy.

PLACES FOR A WINDOW-BOX

Where there is no opportunity to enjoy gardening elsewhere, the window-box presents a medium in which horticultural skill in food growing may be enjoyed to the full. There is a tendency to look upon window-boxes as being no more than containers to hold pots of flowering plants, yet nothing could be farther from the truth, for a window-box of even the smallest proportions can remain productive throughout the year. It is not necessary for a window-box to be fixed in front of a window. If made to the length of the window, a box may be fixed inside the window of a kitchen or living room and in it may be grown chives and thyme, mustard and cress, lettuce and radishes. Boxes, too, may be fixed to the walls of a courtyard and where the walls are 6-8 ft. high, a double row of boxes may be fixed, the lower boxes at about 4 ft. above the ground with the upper ones about 18 in. above the others and fixed with iron brackets between them. Here may be grown dwarf herbs and lettuce, radishes and spring onions, whilst nasturtiums planted in spring at the front of the boxes will trail down and be a blaze of colour all summer, the leaves being used in salads or sandwiches and the seeds pickled green as a substitute for capers, whilst the flowers will brighten the dullest courtyard. The upper boxes may be tended from a step-ladder; this includes their watering, which must be done regularly.

Where it is not practical to fix the boxes to a wall, they may be placed along the bottom of a sunny wall, end to end in a long row. To preserve the wood, raise them on bricks or short lengths of wood so that they will be about 2 in. above ground. If a stone retaining wall has been built at the foot of a courtyard wall, boxes can be placed in front and their use will give additional room for other crops. Similar boxes may be placed at the front and along the sides of a terrace or verandah, those at the front possibly being filled with flowering plants to give colour – geraniums in summer and dwarf tulips and other bulbs during winter and spring – and the side boxes being used for vegetables.

When making the boxes it is essential that they are not too shallow. A depth of 6 in. is advisable and 5 in. is the minimum, so that the roots of the plants will not dry out too quickly in summer, which would necessitate twice daily watering. The deeper the box the more labour-saving it will be, especially where a number of boxes are being used and watering is an important factor. Anything that will reduce watering to a minimum must be done, the careful preparation of the soil and the making up of the box contributing to this in no small way. To some extent the size of box will be dictated by the size of the window, for the box must be to scale or it will detract from the appearance of the property. The large windows of a Georgian house will permit the window-box to be made 8 in. deep, whereas the long, low, mullioned window of a cottage will mean that the box must be made no more than 6 in. deep. The length, too, will be determined by the length of the window. Where boxes are being fixed to the wall of a courtyard or merely placed on blocks around a paved terrace, a verandah or yard, they may be of any reasonable size depending upon where they are to be placed. Long, narrow boxes could be used around the sides of a yard or terrace in place of tubs, where space is strictly limited.

Making the Box

As a window-box has to carry a considerable weight of soil, it should be constructed of 1 in. timber cut to the correct lengths and planed. The front and back of the box should be cut to the length required, the ends fitting inside. When cutting the ends, allow for the thickness of the wood so as to keep to the correct overall measurements required. If any attempt is made to dovetail the corners it should be remembered that the strength of a

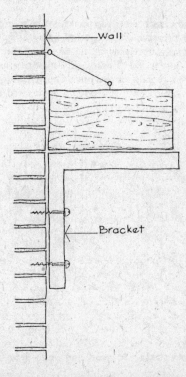

dovetail lies in the perfection of its construction, and a water-resistant glue should be used. When securing the two ends no advantage will be gained by using screws instead of 2 in. nails, for when driven in they only tend to part the grain and split the wood. For additional strength at the corners an angle bracket should be screwed either on the inside or outside of the box.

Adequate drainage holes must be made in the base, about a dozen or so holes of $\frac{1}{2}$ in. diameter rather than half the number of 1 in. diameter, to ensure that there will be little of the compost escaping. Where possible always use hard wood, such as seasoned oak, in the construction of the box, or failing that, American Red Cedar, both of which will remain almost impervious to moisture through the years and neither of which require painting as a preservative.

After the box has been made up it must be treated on the inside with a wood preservative, Cuprinol being efficient. This treatment is especially necessary if the box has been constructed of deal or other soft wood. Thoroughly soak the inside of the box and allow it to remain in the open after treating for at last ten days until it has become thoroughly weathered and any fumes which might be injurious to plant life will have escaped. The box

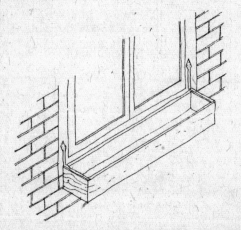

Window box held in position by iron brackets

may then be painted on the outside only, to conform to one's tastes, or to the colour scheme of the house. Against stone or mullioned windows, however, a box made of oak presents a better appearance if it is not painted.

Owing to the weight of soil the boxes are always fixed before they are filled, though it is preferable to add the drainage materials first. And always remember to place the boxes where they can be easily attended. To place them in some inaccessible position which necessitates the use of a pair of steps to give them attention, or where the watering-can has to be held at arm's length above one's head, will be to make window-box gardening a toil rather than a pleasure.

Filling the Box

Before placing any compost in the boxes it will be necessary to ensure thorough drainage. First the drainage holes in the base must be made so that the soil does not fall through, and this is best done by placing a piece of fine mesh wire netting over the base. Then add a layer of crocks to a depth of about half an inch to ensure efficient drainage during winter. Over the crocks, a layer of turves placed grass downwards will occupy another $1\frac{1}{2}$ in. of the box. The remaining space, depending upon the depth of the box, is filled with prepared compost.

The soil should preferably be taken from pasture, or be a good quality loam from a country garden, and where the soil is not troubled by deposits of soot and sulphur. Soil taken from a town garden will generally be of an acid nature and will also contain a large number of weed seeds.

A satisfactory compost will be made up by mixing: three parts loam, one part peat, one part grit or coarse sand (by weight). Allow two pounds of ground limestone or lime rubble to a box 3 ft. long and 6 in. deep; four ounces of bone meal, a slow-acting fertilizer and a sprinkling of superphosphate which encourages a vigorous root action.

It is important to make up a well-drained, friable compost, yet it must also be able to retain moisture during dry periods in summer. For this reason peat or decayed manure, or a little of both, should not be omitted, and where the loam is of a light, sandy nature, then a larger proportion of humus materials should be added. It is necessary to keep the compost sweet as long as possible without continually changing the soil, and for this reason lime in some form should not be omitted. A few pieces of charcoal in the soil will also help to maintain sweetness. Correctly prepared, the compost will not only make for healthy and vigorous plant growth, but will require changing only once every three years.

The window-boxes, after they have been made secure, should be filled several days before they are to be planted so that the compost is allowed time to settle down. The compost is best taken to the boxes in a small bucket, and as it is placed in the box it should be pressed around the sides so that all air pockets are eliminated. The box should be filled to the top and then be allowed three or four days in which to settle down before any planting is done. By this time the compost will have sunk to about half an inch below the top of the box, which will allow for watering without the soil splashing over the side.

Fixing the Box

The correct fixing of the window-box is important and here again this will be governed by the structure. A window with a wooden frame will present few difficulties provided the box is made to the exact dimensions of the frame. Here, a strong iron bracket may be fixed to the top of the sides of the box and to the frame of the window, and in this way the box made quite secure. This is most important, for it must be remembered that a window-box filled with soil amounts to a considerable weight, especially when the soil is wet. There must also be no danger to those walking below, either through the box falling or through falling soil. Remember that wherever the box is fixed, it must permit the opening of the window as well as the watering and planting of the box without undue difficulty. Owing to the considerable weight of a box when filled, it should be fixed into position when empty, boxes which are easily reached being filled from outside, those fixed to an upper room window being filled from inside.

Where a box has to be fixed to a stone or brick wall into which the brackets are to be fastened, the wall must first be plugged to a depth of not less than 2 in. into which the screws are fixed. To give added efficiency in making the box secure, strong galvanized wires should be fastened from the outer edge of the box sides to a position on the wall above the bracket. This will take some of the strain of a box in which may be growing winter and spring flowering plants and which may have become unduly heavy through continuous rain or a fall of snow.

A wooden box is preferable to one of concrete as it is lighter, and more easily constructed and fixed. A wooden box made of 1 in. timber, treated on the inside with preservative and painted on the outside will prove extremely long lasting.

Care of the Box

By early April the boxes should be ready for planting and all that will be necessary is to keep the surface of the soil stirred and comfortably moist in dry weather. The plants will also benefit from a syringe when the weather is warm and this is best given in the evening. When watering in summer, give the compost a thorough soaking so that the water reaches right down to the roots and they do not have to turn to the surface in search of it. If the box is to be left unattended for longer than usual, the soil should first be given a thorough soaking and small flat stones should then be pressed in between the plants. This will prevent too rapid evaporation during a hot period. During August, most plants will benefit from an occasional watering with liquid manure, obtainable from most seedsmen in concentrated form. A small watering-can with a long spout will make for easier watering of window-boxes and hanging baskets; no more than a gallon of water should be handled at one time, or the simple task of watering will prove onerous,

It should be said that those plants to be grown in window-boxes must be suited to the position of the box. For example, in a box with a southerly aspect, French beans and tomatoes can be grown and will crop well there. So will lettuce, which is also suitable for a box facing west. Where the box faces east or north, then only those plants able to withstand cooler conditions and make do with only a little sunshine should be planted. Chives will do well, and parsley. These plants may spend their entire life in 3 in. pots, to be taken indoors in late October and placed in or near the kitchen window to provide flavouring all winter. The boxes may then be planted with primroses and dwarf bulbs to flower in spring.

The culture of window-boxes does call for some thought in their planning to keep them constantly productive, and some effort is needed in their planting. However, it will be worth it for those who have to live on a low fixed income or a pension, where every penny saved will count in balancing the budget.

SINKS AND TROUGHS

Vegetables may also be grown in an old sink, often obtained from builders' merchants for nothing but its removal, whilst an old stone trough with its considerable depth of soil will grow tomatoes, marrows and ridge cucumbers if it is placed in a sheltered, sunny corner. I once grew a splendid crop of mushrooms at the bottom of a stone trough. The growing medium was elephant manure obtained from a circus and the mushrooms were of elephantine proportions when they appeared. An old door was placed over the top of the trough to keep out the rain, for mushrooms are so easily spoiled by excessive wet. The cover also provided the dark conditions which mushrooms enjoy and the thick stone walls of the trough kept it cool inside. Though few will have an old stone trough to hand, one may be made from cement to simulate old stone without any great expense.

Construction of a Trough

The most satisfactory way of constructing a concrete trough is to make two boxes of matured timber, making one about 1½ in. smaller in all dimensions. The smaller box will fit inside the other. For the base and walls of the trough, mix up two parts of sand to one part of cement, adding sufficient water to make it into a paste so that it will pour, though at the same time it must not be too sloppy. The cement should be poured inside the first box to a depth of 1½ in. two large corks being fixed in position to provide the drainage holes. To reinforce the base and sides, a length of wire netting should be pressed into the cement mixture just before it begins to set; this should extend almost to the top of the sides. A second piece of netting should be pressed into the mixture so that it extends up the other two sides in a similar way.

Use 2 in. mesh netting, cutting the pieces to the exact measurement of the mould. Thus for a box 30 in. long by 18 in. wide by 6 in. deep, the two pieces of netting will measure 42 in. and 30 in. The smaller box does not require a base; just make the four sides and hold them together by small pieces of wood nailed across each corner and long enough to stretch across the corners of the first box to prevent it pressing into the concrete base. The cement is then poured between the two boxes. Insert a piece of stick to hold the netting away from the mould and prevent it showing when the concrete has finally set hard, which it will do in about twenty-four hours if not made too thin. Just before the cement has set completely, the sides of the boxes are carefully removed, the inner mould being left in position until it is thoroughly hardened.

The trough or sink should then be filled with a strong solution of permanganate of potash which will neutralize the cement, making it suitable for filling with compost. Allow the solution to remain in the trough for several days, then remove the corks in the base and drain off.

A glazed sink which is to be used for a trough garden should be chipped on the inside as much as possible so that the sink will be more porous, and the roots of the plants will be able to hug the sides in the same way as do plants in earthenware pots. For the same reason plants growing in old stone and concrete troughs have a vigorous root action and as a result, top growth is equally vigorous and healthy.

Making up a Trough

Troughs are heavy, of whatever material they are constructed, so should be given a permanent position before they are prepared for the plants. Make certain that they are quite firm on a single or double pedestal, using wedges where necessary. Over the drainage holes place several large crocks, or pieces of brick or stone, then over the base place a layer of small stones or crocks to a depth of 6 in. Over this lay old turves upside down and then fill to the top with the prepared compost, pressing it well down round the sides. This should be composed of: two parts fresh loam, sterilized if possible; one part top grade peat, which is superior to leaf mould because it contains no weed spores; one part coarse sand and grit. Add a sprinkling of superphosphate to encourage root action, and lime to keep it sweet; also a little bone meal, a slow-acting fertilizer, and mix the whole together. If one has no garden, sterilized loam, peat and sand may readily be obtained from a local nursery, and as a general guide, a barrowful of compost will be required for a sink of approximately 36 in. by 18 in. by 6 in. Most stone troughs are several inches deeper, but rarely more than 24–26 in. in length, so that compost requirements will be much the same. Some troughs have no drainage material, whilst some pieces of broken charcoal should be mixed with the compost to maintain its sweetness.

Food Plants for Window-Box and Trough

Beetroot. For sowing in April, Sutton's Early Bunch is quick to reach tennis ball size after thinning the plants to 2 in. apart. This spacing may be achieved by sowing pelleted seed, thus saving time and labour. All root crops must be kept supplied with moisture in dry weather, otherwise they will grow hard and woody instead of succulent and juicy.

Carrot. The best variety for a window-box is Parisian Rondo which from an April sowing matures quickly, the roots being the size of golf balls and bright orange. They cook quickly and are sweet and juicy. As with other roots, successional sowings may be made every two months from early April. Keep the soil well supplied with decayed manure or used hops.

French Beans. Sow in window-boxes or a trough about mid-April, planting the seeds 5 in. apart; or sow in boxes indoors and plant out mid-May when 2 in. tall. Outstanding for window-boxes is Limelight from Thompson & Morgan which has thick, fibreless beans and crops at least two weeks before any other variety. Make a second sowing in another box towards the end of June and continue the cropping until early September. Other good varieties are Tendergreen and Royalty, whose purple beans turn dark green in boiling water. It is noted for its exceptional flavour.

Herbs. Early spring is the most suitable time to plant dwarf herbs in a window box. Young plants are obtainable from herb farms and will soon begin to make bushy growth. Balm, chives, sweet basil, the various thymes, parsley, marjoram and winter savory are all suitable, for they do not grow more than 12 in. tall. They can be kept tidy and compact by pinching back any long shoots whilst the leaves should be removed judiciously to maintain the balance of the plant as they are required for culinary purposes. The plants will respond to a top dressing twice yearly and syringing with clean water in warm weather.

Herbs are readily increased by root division in spring and by taking and rooting cuttings around the side of a plant pot containing a sandy compost. When rooted, plant them 5 in. apart in the window-box. Parsley should be sown in small pots and transplanted to the box with the soil ball intact.

Kale. The curly Scottish kale makes a most handsome short, bushy plant in a window-box and if planted in June, after taking a crop of carrots or lettuce, the plants will provide many handfuls of leaves to cook throughout winter and early spring when 'greens' are most wanted. Remove and use them when young and succulent.

Lettuce. Tom Thumb, a cabbage variety, is the one for window-boxes. Sow seed in boxes or pans indoors in March and plant out in April, allowing only 5 in. between the plants. It makes a crisp solid head in a month, so have a succession of seedlings ready to plant out all summer and until late October. Lettuces are now no longer cheap in the shops and yet no salad is worthy of its name without them.

For troughs, All the Year Round, to mature as its name implies, is also recommended.

Mustard and Cress. Sow thickly at fortnightly intervals and at one end of a window-box, sowing the cress five days earlier so that both will be ready together. Cut when 2 in. high, using scissors or a sharp knife. Make the first sowing about 1 April and for winter salads, sow indoors from 1 October.

Radish. Sow seed at monthly intervals from early April. Scatter the seed around the seedling lettuces after planting and the radishes will be ready at the same time. Cherry Belle, like a round red cherry, is excellent, as is Scarlet Globe, both having crisp, nutty flesh.

Spring Onions. White Lisbon is the best variety, and a sowing is made in March for pulling midsummer onwards. If a sowing is made in early September the plants will winter unharmed and be ready to pull in April.

Tomato. For a window box plant Tiny Tim at the end of May. It will make a bushy plant less than 18 in. tall yet will bear up to twenty or more trusses, each carrying a handful of sweet and juicy fruits of marble size. If the plants are given a weekly application of dilute manure water, they will continue to crop until the end of October. For troughs, Sleaford Abundance and Red Ensign may be grown. They grow only 2 ft. tall and make bushy plants, capable of bearing many pounds of full-size tomatoes in a season.

Turnip. It may be grown in a trough or box, sowing the seed at six-week intervals from 1 April. Tokio Cross or Golden Perfection will bear turnips of golf ball size within four to five weeks if the plants are thinned to 1 in. apart. Sow a double row to have a worthwhile boiling and sow again after pulling.

CHAPTER FOUR

FOOD FROM TUBS, CONTAINERS AND HANGING BASKETS

Surprisingly few people make use of tubs for growing anything, yet they are so useful for growing fruit and vegetables where there is only a small garden or perhaps no garden at all. Place them around a courtyard or on a terrace or verandah, keeping the size of tub in proportion to the garden feature where they are to be placed. They may be used to grow standard apples and pears and in summer, edged with ivy leaf geraniums and lobelia of trailing habit. Tubs and containers may also be planted with bush tomatoes in summer and with tulips, polyanthus and wallflowers to bloom in spring to give colour when most wanted. When the tubs are cleared in May, the tomatoes will follow. Here again, the tubs may be edged with ivy leaf geraniums and lobelia and it is surprising how colourful they look when the tomatoes are beginning to ripen in July, like rubies against the emerald foliage. Indeed, tomatoes are one of the best of all plants to grow in tubs and containers, and heavy crops will result if the plants have been grown well.

TUBS AND THEIR CARE

The best tubs are those made from cider or vinegar makers' barrels which are of oak and have well fitting ends which will be the base of the tubs after the barrels have been cut in two. They may be obtained from the Taunton Cider Company and from The Barrel House, St. Agnes, Cornwall, whilst there are vinegar makers in various parts of the country who often have for disposal old casks which are usually smaller than those used by cidermakers. If the terrace or verandah is small, tubs of this size are ideal. Tubs are obtainable in all sizes and are very reasonably priced considering that if treated with a wood preservative before filling with soil, both on the inside and outside, they will prove long lasting, with a life of twenty or more years. The iron rims should also be treated with a rust-proof preparation, for these are always first to perish. They should then be painted black. With the weathered oak and black rims, tubs look most handsome wherever used.

To be effective, tubs should be of not less than 18 in. diameter and 15 in. high, but they may be up to 22 in. in diameter and 18 in. high, which is a suitable size for a large courtyard. The greater the amount of soil the tubs will hold, the less amount of moisture evaporation there will be and so less need for watering in the summer. The tubs should be drilled at the base with three or four holes of about 1 in. diameter to allow surplus moisture to drain away in winter, otherwise the soil in the tubs will quickly turn sour.

Where oak tubs are not readily obtainable, a plastic terrace tub designed by Mr. Martyn Rowlands F.S.I.A. and made in simulated stone finish by Harcostar Garden Products is light to handle and is weatherproof and long lasting. Of 24 in. diameter and 14 in. high, it looks remarkably effective in a large courtyard or on a terrace of ample proportions.

For a verandah, there is the smaller 'Abbey' plant tub made of polythene to the colour of old oak and with the Tudor rose and fleur-de-lis motifs, which is 12 in. in diameter and $10\frac{1}{2}$ in. deep. Of similar size is the Purbeck 'tub' in polythene, also with a simulated stone finish and made by Geeco Products. Priced at little more than £1 each, they will give years of service.

Plants may be grown in large earthenware pots or in those made from expanded polystyrene, the Flair range which includes the Barrel pot, having a stone finish. Of $8\frac{1}{2}$ in. diameter, it is 9 in. high and because of its wide base, is not readily blown over.

Moisture Requirements

It is important to provide all plants with sufficient moisture, lack of which is the chief cause of failure with fruit trees especially in pots or tubs. Lack of moisture will prevent the fruit from reaching its normal size; it will lack flavour and may not store well, or may fall long before it is mature.

Any plant growing in a pot or tub will dry out at the roots during the period June to September far more quickly than where growing in the open ground, which may be provided with a mulch to retain moisture in the soil, as well as the roots being able to search more freely for food and moisture. It must also be remembered that a tree in a pot or tub will have its roots subjected to the almost unprotected rays of the hot summer sun. It is therefore important to give protection for the plants and during May straw, strawy manure or sacking should be packed around the pots and kept damp. This will protect the pots from the rays of the sun and so prevent a too rapid loss of moisture from the soil.

If growing in pots it is a good idea to fix a 10 in. board along the base of the wall 18 in. away from it. This will form a trough to take the pots, the space around each pot being filled in with peat. Clean to use, it may be kept continually moist; or soil may be used to surround the pots. The pots should be placed on a 2-3 in. layer of ashes or peat which may also be placed over the soil of the pots to act as a mulch. An alternative mulch for those living in or near the country is one of strawy farmyard or stable manure, though this will not be so clean to handle as peat.

Throughout the summer months the roots must be constantly supplied with moisture, a thorough watering being given almost daily, so that the moisture may reach the bottom of the pot. The peat or soil around the pots must also be kept moist. To allow the soil in the pots to dry out for only a short period will cause irreparable damage to the plants.

Food Plants for Pots and Tubs

APPLES AND PEARS

Where growing apples and pears in pots, it is usual to grow them as cordons and, in this way, the maximum number of different varieties can be grown. This will help with pollination where bees and other insects may be less prevalent in industrial town gardens. The cordons are supported by stout canes, which when growing against a wall will be held in place by strong wires.

These are looped around each cane and fastened to the wall by a strong nail at intervals of 6-7 ft.

Where a wall, especially a sunny wall, can be provided, this will prove ideal for fruits, for not only will the trees be protected from strong and cold winds, but the fruit will ripen and colour better than it would where growing in the open ground. If a wall cannot be provided and the plants are to grow unprotected, it will be better to grow several dwarf pyramids in tubs, for they will be better able to withstand strong winds.

Besides the need for care to be taken in the selection of suitable pollinators, the most suitable trees will be those which form close spurs, rather than those which bear fruit on the tips of the branches which are the most vigorous growers.

Apples in Order of Ripening

Duchess of Oldenburg	(August)
Lady Sudeley	(August)
Ellison's Orange	(September)
Michaelmas Red	(September)
Egremont Russet	(October)
Sunset	(November)
King of the Pippins	(December)
Adam's Pearmain	(December to January)
Claygate Pearmain	(December to March)
May Queen	(April to June)

Though Lady Sudeley is a tip bearer, it bears its fruit on very short twigs or shoots so that it may be said to come somewhere between the tip and spur bearers and is very suitable for pot culture.

Pears in Order of Ripening

Laxton's Superb	(August)
Beurré Bedford	(September)
Gorham	(September)
Conference	(October)
Louise Bonne	(November)
Glou Morceau	(December)
Roosevelt	(December to January)
Santa Claus	(December to February)
Bergamotte d'Esperen	(February to March)

Planting

A very large pot or small tub should be used for fruit trees so that the roots are not unduly restricted and can obtain the maximum food from the compost. Crocks or broken brick should be placed at the bottom of each so that the drainage holes are kept open and over these should be placed a small quantity of fresh turf loam. Do not use ordinary soil as found in a town garden for this is usually sour and lacking in nutriment.

Carefully remove the tap root and trim off any other unduly large roots before placing the trees in the pots or tubs, spreading out the roots.

The compost should consist of turf loam to which has been added a small quantity of old mushroom bed manure, or well decayed farmyard manure, but not too much, for an excess of nitrogen must be guarded against otherwise the trees will make too much wood and foliage. Potash is important; a quarter of an ounce of sulphate of potash should be allowed for each pot and must be thoroughly worked into the compost. This should be friable so that it may may be carefully packed round the roots and the pot filled to within 1 in. of the rim.

It is not necessary to wait for the ending of the usual winter frosts before planting if the compost is made up indoors (in a cellar or shed); planting may be done any time from mid-November until mid-March, but the six weeks before Christmas is the best time. This will enable the trees to become thoroughly settled in before coming into bloom in late spring.

Culture

The care of the trees will be carried out on the same lines as described for trees trained into the artificial form (See Chapter 2), but help should be given with the setting of the blossom by dusting the individual blooms with a camel-hair brush during dry days, and on several occasions at flowering time. If suitable pollinators are also planted together, there should then be a heavy set of fruit.

Help may also be given to the trees to satisfy their moisture requirements by frequent syringing of the foliage, from early June onwards, but if this is done whilst the trees are still in bloom, it must be done in time for the moisture to have dried off before nightfall, as damage might be done by late frosts if the blooms are wet.

The trees will also benefit if they are fed once each week with diluted liquid manure water from early July when the fruit is beginning to swell. This should be continued until the end of September for the sake of the trees as well as the fruit.

Where growing in a sheltered position, the fruit of later ripening varieties may be allowed to hang almost until Christmas, being removed as it is required, and only that of the very late maturing varieties will need to be stored for use in the new year. This should be removed by the third week of December, when the trees growing in pots are re-potted. This is done about every third year into a freshly made up compost. Trees in tubs which contain a larger quantity of compost and provide more nourishment, may be allowed to remain without re-potting for a good number of years, if systematically fed and never allowed to suffer lack of moisture. During winter the trees will require no artificial watering, but this may be necessary in April, possibly after a long period of frost and drying winds.

STRAWBERRIES

Where space is limited, fresh strawberries may be grown in tubs or barrels, into which holes 1 in. in diameter and 18 in. apart have been drilled to take the plants. The tubs should be filled with a suitable compost, and a small courtyard or verandah could possibly accommodate several tubs or barrels, so that a succession of fruit can be enjoyed. Tubs are preferable, for if planted in the usual way all the plants may be given abundant moisture. This is essential if the plants around the sides are to fruit well.

The half-barrel or tub must be drilled with drainage holes, over which are placed large crocks then a layer of turf, grass side downwards. Then fill the tub to within 1 in. of the rim with fresh loam enriched with some decayed manure, peat, a small amount of coarse sand, and a handful of bone meal to each tub. The ingredients should have been mixed well together and allowed to settle down before planting takes place in autumn, or in March if the autumn fruiting varieties are being grown. If placed in a warm corner, an early June crop may be enjoyed. The compost must never be allowed to lack moisture. In May, give

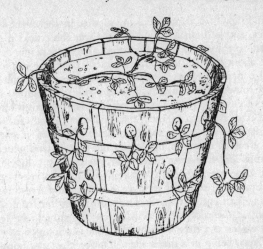

Strawberries in a tub.

the compost a soaking each week, so that the moisture will percolate to those plants situated at the base of the tub but not so that
water will run out at the bottom. An occasional watering with
liquid manure will help the formation of large, richly flavoured
fruits.

Strawberries may also be grown in large pots. They require
the same compost as for tubs, but will need additional moisture,
for compost in pots will dry out quickly in early summer and it
may be necessary to water twice daily. Pot-grown plants may be
purchased early in March; they will be more expensive than
runners, but will bear fruit the same season and may also be
retained to fruit the following year. If there is garden space to
grow on runners, planting them in early autumn, or if runners
can be planted and grown-on in small pots, this will be less expensive.

TOMATOES
Bush tomatoes crop heavily in tubs, taking advantage of the considerable depth of soil to form masses of fibrous roots. Holes are
drilled in the base, over which is placed a layer of crocks or

broken brick to a depth of 2 in. so that in the event of wet weather, ample drainage is available. Over the crocks is placed decayed turf loam mixed with some decayed manure which should about half fill the tub. The balance will be of prepared compost, depending much upon the requirements of the plants that are to occupy the tubs. As a general rule, the compost should consist of new turf loam, for the soil of town gardens is often inert and acid. As the compost is usually left in the tubs for several years, it must be well prepared. Kettering loam is excellent where it can be obtained, but loam from pasture land which will be fibrous and free from weed spores is equally valuable. Mix with it some peat, especially where the soil is of a heavy nature. A well prepared soil will produce a healthy and free-flowering plant and will ensure that the plants do not suffer from lack of moisture at the roots. This will enable the tubs to be left for several weeks at a time without the plants coming to any great harm. Also, being in a more open situation than a window-box and covering a greater surface area, tubs are better able to take up natural moisture by way of dew and rain.

Before filling, the tubs should be raised on pieces of wood, bricks or stones of about 2 in. thickness and should be made quite secure so that they cannot tilt. This will greatly prolong the life of the tubs by keeping the base above ground level, providing a circulation of air and preventing the tubs remaining for long in pools of rain-water.

After the tubs have been filled to the brim with the prepared compost, allow a full week for it to settle down before planting. By the time it has done so it will leave about 2 in. from the soil level to the top of the tub, which will allow for watering and for a top dressing to be given where necessary, and also prevent water from being splashed over the sides by heavy rain.

To prevent the soil from becoming sour, it should be given a top dressing with lime each year when the tomatoes are cleared. This, together with the careful preparation of the soil, should give the compost a life of at least four years before refilling is necessary. A small amount of crushed charcoal mixed into the compost will also help to keep it sweet for charcoal absorbs the gases given off by the manure.

The bush tomato should be grown in tubs; plant those

suggested for frame and cloche culture. French Cross and Pixie make bushy plants 2-3 ft. tall, so plant three or four to a tub of 20 in. diameter and edge it with trailing lobelia or dwarf French marigolds to give additional colour. If small pots or other containers of about 8-9 in. diameter are being used, plant one tomato to each. For this purpose, plant Tiny Tim, which makes a bush 18 in. tall and bears masses of small tomatoes throughout summer. Short twigs placed about the foliage will prevent the plants from being damaged in strong wind. They do not require stopping.

Plants may be raised in a propagator in February and grown-on in pots in a sunny kitchen window or warm greenhouse to be planted in the tubs in late May in the south or June in the north when they will be showing the first truss of bloom.

After planting, top dress with a 1 in. layer of decayed manure and keep the plants supplied with water. A weekly application of dilute manure water will increase the yield and quality, whilst dusting the flowers with a camel hair brush when they are dry will help to ensure a heavy set of fruit, especially with the first trusses. By mid-July, the first fruits will have ripened and the plants will continue to ripen their fruit until late October, when they should be removed from the tubs and replaced with tulips and wallflowers to flower in spring, or plant them with winter lettuce.

HERBS

Herbs are admirable plants for tub culture, in fact no other plants give such an old world charm to oak tubs. If there is room for only one tub or perhaps two, then herbs should be used to fill them. Placed by the side of a doorway, the plants may easily be reached even during adverse weather whilst being evergreen, they are not only interesting but useful in the kitchen the whole year through.

Prepare the tub as described for tomatoes, though herbs do not require so rich a soil. The best time to make up the tubs is early in spring, so that the plants will have the summer months to make plenty of growth and become established. At the centre of the tub, plant rosemary, lemon balm, hyssop and sage, with a tree onion or two for flavouring. Around these, plant chives or the stouter growing Welsh onions, also the different culinary thymes, together with marjoram and winter savory. Around the edge, sow parsley seed which will provide its densely curled leaves for garnishing or sauces throughout the year, and will last at least two years if the flower stems are removed before they set seed. Parsley sown in this way will even enhance a tub of scarlet geraniums.

The herbs will be longer-lasting and produce a greater abundance of leaf (which is what is required of them) if the flower heads are removed as they form. Correctly planned, a complete herb garden may be planted in a tub and all the attention it requires is to keep the soil stirred so that it does not 'pan' after heavy rain and to give an occasional top dressing with a mixture of peat and decayed manure which will keep the plants vigorous and healthy.

If a second tub is to be planted with herbs, plant tarragon and tansy, also sweet cecily and rue, with its blue-green foliage, at the centre. Here, too, sow a few seeds of the annual borage, with its flowers of brilliant blue and leaves which lend their refreshing cucumber flavour to Pimm's No. 1 and other summer drinks, cider especially. Dr Fernie, the authority on herbal remedies during Victorian times, said that the reputed powers of invigoration could be entirely substantiated for borage as the juice contains thirty per cent nitrate of potash. There is an old Latin adage which, when translated, reads 'I, Borage, bring always courage' and John Pechey, writing during the Restoration, said 'the distilled water and the conserve of the flowers, comfort the heart, relieve the faint, clear the melancholy, and purify the blood'. Enjoy the leaves with cream cheese in sandwiches or fry them in batter, cover with melted cheese and have brown bread to accompany them.

Leaves of salad burnet, too, are delicious in sandwiches with cheese or can be used in a salad. The plant may be set around the side of a tub with a few trailing nasturtiums in between. Like those of watercress, nasturtium leaves are rich in compounds of iron and sulphur and may be used in a salad, but do so sparingly for they have a wholesome bitterness. The seeds, too, when pickled are an excellent substitute for capers. Gather them whilst green, place in a wide-topped bottle or jar and pour over them malt vinegar (a pint to every pound of seed) which has been boiled with half an ounce of salt and one or two peppercorns, then allow to cool and place in a dark cupboard for at least two months before using the seed as an accompaniment to fish. Their slightly bitter flavour is most enjoyable.

FOOD FROM HANGING BASKETS

Herbs may also be grown in a hanging basket fixed to the wall of a house or courtyard, where they provide colour and interest all the year round. Two or three baskets, fixed to the wall with wrought-iron brackets so that the bottom of the baskets are just above head height, may be watered and tended by means of a small step-ladder. Only during long periods of drought will watering be necessary, for herbs enjoy dry conditions. They may be planted (in the south) with nasturtiums which will trail down informally, adding their own particular charm to the display with their brilliant colour and will in no way interfere with the herbs. The baskets may also be suspended from the eaves of a bungalow or between rustic poles, possibly to divide one part of the garden from another, where three or four baskets will be most effective. The herbs require sunlight so do not place the baskets in the shade. Large hooks will be needed to hang the baskets beneath the eaves of a house, whilst they may be suspended from a wall by driving in a strong iron stake, cementing it in.

A basket of suitable size will be of 18-20 in. diameter, made of galvanized iron so that it can be expected to have a long life. A smaller basket, made of green plastic-coated steel, may also be used if the courtyard is small, whilst it will be ideal to hang in a garden or sunroom where herbs will behave admirably and will always be on hand to use in the kitchen.

To absorb moisture and to prevent soil from falling through the basket, line it with moss obtained from nearby woodlands or hedgerows, or from a garden shop. Make a thick layer and have it comfortably moist, then put in the soil. This should be sterilized loam to which has been added a sprinkling of bone meal or steamed bone flour. Also mix in some peat and a little decayed manure. Prepare the baskets early in spring, placing the base over a large pot or a box to keep it stable and leaving it for a week or so after planting. This is to allow the plants to become established

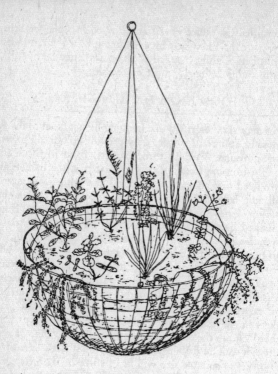

Herbs in a hanging basket.

before the baskets go out, where they will have to contend with winds. They should go out about 1 April. If a little crushed charcoal is added, this will keep the soil sweet. As the baskets will be undisturbed for some time, attention to detail in their making will be advisable.

The Elizabethan custom of having pots of fragrant herbs in the rooms of the house is a delightful one. Rosemary always does well suspended above a sunny window and stays green all the year, keeping the room fragrant with its refreshing resinous smell, whilst sprigs may be used in cooking. During summer, put the baskets outside for two to three months, when the plants will respond to sunlight and fresh air by making vigorous new growth. The basket is lifted down for watering once a week when it is placed in the kitchen sink and there left to drain overnight.

Around the side of the baskets plant several ground ivy, the ale-hoof of country inns and old cottage gardens, for its leaves were in constant demand to clarify beer before the introduction of hops. It is a delightful plant for window-boxes, too, the creeping stems trailing over the side, the heart-shaped leaves being grey-green, marked and edged with purple and white whilst the tiny purple flowers are borne at the axils of the leaves.

At the centre of the basket plant hyssop, all parts of which are fragrant. So often mentioned in the Bible, it became known as the Holy herb. The flowers and leaves have a pleasant sharp taste in stews. Near it, set a root of sweet marjoram, a plant, like hyssop, to be found in every Tudor garden. The leaves, like those of the native common marjoram, were used in stuffings and to flavour soups and could with advantage be more often used today.

The fragrant thymes, woody plants growing 5-6 in. tall, should find a place in every hanging basket, the lemon-scented variety being especially useful. And a few roots of chives to cut all winter, to sprinkle over omelettes, could also be included. Regular removal of the shoots for kitchen use will keep the plants compact.

The indispensable parsley should be sown in pots which are hung on an outside wall near the kitchen door.

CHAPTER FIVE

FOOD FROM THE BORDER

There is no finer feature in the garden than a well-stocked herbaceous border such as could at one time be found in the gardens of most large houses. But as gardens are small now and the herbaceous border needs time spent on staking the plants and cleaning it in autumn, it has largely been replaced with ornamental shrubs or roses. Yet they do not have so long a flowering season as a border of hardy plants which will bloom almost the whole year round.

Where a border is already established it should not be disturbed but even so, in the several bare places which are usually caused by plants dying off in winter or from old age, those vegetables which have attractive foliage could be planted amongst the herbaceous plants, and possibly also a number of herbs such as fennel and rue, both admired for their interesting leaf patterns as well as for their other valuable qualities. There are several vegetables which always seem more at home in a mixed border than they do in the vegetable garden and are just as easily managed there, though the border needs to be in a sunny situation, not overhung by mature trees which tend to deprive the plants of light and moisture. Vegetables require similar conditions to those provided for them when grown as specialized crops.

GLOBE ARTICHOKE

One vegetable that will add distinction to any border is the globe artichoke, native of the North African coastline and one of the oldest of cultivated plants. It is first recorded in Britain during Tudor times and was one of Charles I's favourite foods, so much so that his Irish cook, Joseph Cooper, conjured up many ideas of how to serve the vegetable to his royal master to give him most enjoyment. One way was to slice the succulent heads upwards from the base and to fry the slices in batter. Served with orange juice or slices of orange, it is especially delicious when accompanying roast duckling.

The plant likes some degree of comfort in its growing conditions if it is to be long living. It enjoys a mild climate and a light, well-drained sandy soil, to remind it of its native land, but exceptional heat is not necessary. It will grow well south of the Trent but always grows best near the coast, where it can be provided with chopped seaweed for the humus it needs in summer, though any other form of humus is equally valuable. Old mushroom bed compost or used brewery hops are ideal.

It makes a bushy plant 3-4 ft. tall, its handsomely divided grey-green leaves resembling those of the acanthus, and terminating to a point. Established plants bear their globular heads of the size of a large orange (do not let them grow larger or they will be tough) in midsummer, but suckers planted in November will not usually bear heads before early autumn of the following year. Suckers appear around the parent plant in spring, and may also be planted then. If several are removed each year and grown-on, older plants can be discarded after about four years, for it is when the plants are young that the heads are most succulent.

Remove the suckers when they are 6-8 in. tall, using a knife to sever them from the parent plant. Try to remove each one with a few roots attached for this will help it to grow away quickly. Plant 3 ft. apart, as each plant, in its second year, needs a square yard to develop, for it will grow bushy and will send up numerous 'globes', which are the flower heads, each season. Set the shoots (suckers) 3-4 in. deep into a friable soil and water them in. The plants will appreciate a mulch of decayed manure and lawn mowings each summer, which will act as plant food and will help to retain moisture in the soil. Also, give a top dressing with strawy manure in late autumn, after the foliage has died down and has been removed. This is done when the border is made tidy for winter. If the garden is exposed, heap some soil over the straw mulch to give the plants protection. If the winter frosts are severe, cover the roots with bracken, wood shavings or boiler ash for additional protection.

In summer, never allow the plants to lack moisture, otherwise the 'globes' will become tough and stringy. They must have moisture to be succulent, when they will be rich in vitamins and mineral salts. During June and July, the plants will benefit from an occasional application of dilute manure water whilst early in spring, sprinkle half an ounce of sodium nitrate around each plant. Done on a wet day, this will help them to get away to a good start.

Remove the heads before they become too large, at the same time removing about half of the stem. A guide for cutting will be when the 'globes' are of the size of a large orange but the scales have not begun to open. As soon as they have been cut, trim off the spines and steam the heads for an hour at least. Then remove the centre, fill with prepared mushrooms, egg or tomatoes and serve hot with a suitable sauce.

The plant is troubled neither by pest nor disease. Two varieties are available, the Green and the Purple. The former is superior as to flavour and quality but is more difficult to obtain. It is named Vert de Laon and the scales are virtually spineless. One of the few nurseries still to have it is John Scott & Co., of Merriott, Somerset. Plant it towards the back of a border and near it grow fennel with its finely divided foliage like filigree lace, a herb used for sauces to accompany fish since mediaeval times. Also from France comes Grande Beurré which makes a large head with a large amount of fleshy scales. Boiled and served with melted butter, it is delicious.

The bronze-leaved variety should also be grown and looks particularly attractive with white phlox nearby.

In a light soil, the plant, which is perennial, grows 4-5 ft. tall, though it can be kept lower and bushier by the frequent removal of the top stems to use in the kitchen. Allow each plant about 2 sq. ft. of ground and give it a soil containing a little decayed manure.

SAGE AND OTHER HERBS

No border is complete without its purple flowering sages, so too should it contain those grown for their scented leaf qualities

They are entirely at home in the border though their flowers are not so conspicuous. *Salvia officinalis* is the sage used in stuffings, the broad-leaved form being the best; its pungent leaves are of the grey-green colour associated with this plant. It grows about 2 ft. tall and quite bushy, so plant it towards the centre of the border. There are also several colourful varieties which grow about 15 in. tall and which should be planted to the front. The golden-leaf form has foliage of a lovely soft shade of greenish gold, whilst Tricolor has leaves which are splashed with purple, pink and white. The variety *purpurea* has purple leaves and stems.

A delightful plant for the front of the border is the salad burnet; its tiny leaves, which appear in fern-like fronds, make a pleasing addition to summer salads, whilst its little brownish-green flower heads are most interesting. Growing only 12 in. tall, the leaves have a slight cucumber smell and taste.

Two or three plants in a little group, set 12 in. apart, will provide sufficient leaves to impart their flavour to a salad all the year. Remove a few from each plant when required.

The pot marjoram, *Origanum onites,* also grows to a similar height, its leaves having a refreshing minty taste and smell. Sprinkle the chopped leaves on scrambled eggs or omelettes, or over a Welsh rarebit, and into soups; it also makes a delicious sauce to have with fish.

French tarragon, of similar habit and also a perennial, is used in the same way in soups and may be used with all egg dishes. 'Tarragon eggs' have long been a favourite meal for country folk – hard boiled eggs covered with grated carrots and sprinkled with either fresh or dry tarragon leaves. Serve with a dressing made of salad oil and tarragon vinegar, seasoned with salt and pepper.

Artemesia dracunculus, the French tarragon, is however rather too tender to grow north of the Trent so should be confined to southern gardens. In the north, plant the closely related Russian tarragon which is hardier and grows 3-4 ft. tall. It is a handsome plant, with its finely cut foliage, to have at the back of a border and is used in the same way as the French variety though has not so delicate a flavour.

Lemon balm grows to a similar height and with its fresh lemony scent and flavour is used in stuffings to accompany poultry, or in a mushroom omelette, and to make sauces to accompany fish. There is a dwarf golden-leaf form, not nearly so fragrant but making a colourful plant for the front of a border.

At the back of the border, plant sweet cecily, *Myrrhis odorata*, its leaves with their slight aniseed scent being used sparingly in soups and stews, and imparting a unique flavour to stewed fruit.

It is an interesting plant, the thrice-pinnate leaves of palest green being downy whilst the white flowers, borne early in summer are followed by shapely ridged dark brown fruits which have a slight smell of cloves. Countrymen know it as sweet fern for its leaves are like those of the oak fern and when eaten in a salad, taste as if they have been steeped in sugar, yet their slight aniseed flavour decrees that they should be used sparingly until the taste is acquired. The leaves may also be boiled as a substitute for spinach but their flavour is not to everyone's taste.

Until quite recent times, countrymen used the roots grated raw in a salad and served with salad oil, vinegar and pepper; or they were cooked and sliced and eaten with salad dressing. The plant is best raised from seed, sown early in April where it is to grow and thinning to 20 in. apart.

Nor should the lovely rampion be omitted from the border. It is *Campanula rapunculus* and is perennial, growing 2-3 ft. tall with broad ovate leaves, the handsome purple flowers being the largest of the bell-flower family. They appear in June in large erect panicles. The leaves may be used in salads or steamed and served like spinach, whilst the roots can be boiled or braised or grated raw in a winter salad.

Sorrel is one of those old fashioned plants that used to grow in every border, planted to the front, for it is of tufted spreading habit. Farm workers would bind the leaves over open wounds when it would soon bring about their healing. They would also eat it with cheese in sandwiches for the leaves are rich in potash and are most sustaining. They are delicious made into a sauce to serve with duck or pork as a substitute for Bramley apples, taking away the richness and making the meat more readily digested. Cooks called it green sauce and made it by pouring a little vinegar over a handful of leaves, then beating to a fine consistency and adding a teaspoonful of sugar. It adds delightful piquancy to cold meats and interest to fish dishes, with which it is often served in Ireland. An early fourteenth century manuscript in the Sloane Museum suggests sorrel sauce to serve with duck.

If sorrel plants are not allowed to set seed after flowering, they will be fully perennial and make a dense amount of new leaf each year.

The curry plant, *Helichrysum angustifolium*, with its metallic silvery foliage and growing 2 ft. tall, is highly effective to grow in any border for the beauty of its foliage which when pressed releases a pungent scent of curry powder. The leaves can be used fresh in an omelette or to flavour soups, and when dried they add interest to stuffings and stews. It is best grown in those gardens which enjoy a mild winter climate.

MAKING AND STOCKING A FOOD BORDER

There are a great many other edible plants to grow in the permanent border and a good idea is to make a border devoted entirely to them. An open, sunny situation is essential and a friable well-drained soil containing some decayed manure in whatever form available. Work in some peat to retain summer moisture and before planting, make sure that the ground is cleared of perennial weeds.

The food border can be made to any size or shape but, where there is space, make it as large as possible so as to provide the household with a year's supply of vegetables and herbs. I would suggest it be about 6-8 ft. wide for this will allow for several rows of plants, those growing 4-5 ft. tall at the back, and those 2-3 ft. at the centre, with the more compact to the front. Thus if the border faces south or west, each of the plants will receive the maximum amount of sunshine each sunny day. A good-sized border will also enable the plants to be given sufficient room to develop and mature, since vegetables need sunlight and air to come to maturity. With flowers this is not so important as it is with vegetables and herbs.

Planting is best done in spring, beginning in early March as soon as the soil is in suitable condition and completing by the end of April. Before planting, make a diagram of the border and those plants which are to be included. Some will be obtained as plants from nurseries which specialize in them; others will be raised from seed, sown in boxes possibly in a greenhouse or frame, transplanting later to the border; or seed may be sown in the border where the plants are to grow to maturity. Allow each plant or group of plants space to develop, as already mentioned.

There are a number of food plants which have ornamental foliage whilst some could be grown entirely for the beauty and rich colour of their flowers. Besides those already mentioned, to the front of the border plant groups of *Calendula officinalis,* the pot marigold, its orange petals being used since earliest times to flavour soups and stews. The best variety is Radio with its quilled or rolled petals of deepest orange, or its yellow counterpart, Golden Beam. Sow seed in circles of 12 in. diameter and thin the plants to 6 in. apart. They will bloom almost the whole year and will seed themselves so that the first sowing should be the last to be made for some time.

Another annual beautiful in bloom is borage, *Borago officinalis,* its blue flowers visited by bees in their multitudes, its leaves with their refreshing cucumber flavour adding interest to Pimm's No. 1 and cider drinks, whilst they are delicious in brown bread sandwiches to accompany cream cheese. Sow seed in April to the centre of the border, for the plants grow 2-3 ft. tall.

Also a delightful bee plant is chicory or succory. The country-man knew it better by its more familiar name of turnsole for, like the marigold, it always turns its flowers to the sun. Its china-blue flowers appear late in summer. The roots can be forced in the dark in winter as described in the next chapter, but it is also a valuable food plant in that its leaves may be included in salads and also in soups and broths and help to sustain those recovering slowly from long illness.

Chicory is a perennial and as it grows 4-5 ft. tall, it must be planted at the back of a border or at the centre of an island bed. It is a suitable companion for the globe artichoke, Russian tarragon and fennel.

For the centre of a border, there is no lovelier plant than the bergamot, *Monarda didyma.* It was given its common name because its leaves when pressed release the distinct perfume of bergamot orange. Their flowers of red, pink or white are borne in whorls during July and August and the leaves are used in cider and wine drinks, also to make a delicous 'tea', known in Canada as 'Oswego tea' for the plant was first collected at Oswego Bay on Lake Ontario by John Bartram in 1744.

Runner beans may be grown as a backcloth to the border, the emerald leaves and scarlet flowers being attractive in late summer. Grow them up canes in rows or tent fashion, or against a trellis. Allow space in front to gather the beans, then plant all the taller growng vegetables and herbs, with those of less vigorous habit in front of them and so on to the front of the border where clumps of parsley and purslane may be grown, and the dwarf herbs such as thyme and marjoram. Here also may be grown Lamb's Lettuce, an almost prostrate plant with its bright green oblong leaves so useful for winter salads. The young leaves are widely used in France in spring and it was the Huguenot refugees of Elizabethan times who first drew our attention to their culinary value.

Plant chives in clumps, also to the front of the border. They take up little space and one may cut them all the year, to flavour omelettes and other egg dishes, also stews and soups. Chives and parsley are so full of vitamins and mineral salts that a dish each should be on every table for lunch and supper on every day of the year, to be sprinkled over meats and vegetables.

Another valuable salad plant for early summer is lady's smock, the mauve flowers appearing in April, arising on 15 in. stems from a rosette of pinnate leaves. We know it only as a flower of damp meadows, its presence heralding the summer, but its leaves have the same appetizing bitterness as watercress and may be used in the same way, with cream cheese in sandwiches and in a salad. So health-giving are the leaves, that in olden times they were eaten in large quantities when fish was the staple diet. The plant is of interest in that it will reproduce itself from the tiny plantlets which appear on the leaves. If detached and placed on top of a box of soil, they will form sturdy plants to bloom next year. It is fully perennial. So too is Good King Henry, a plant of the hedgerow. Again, it was the French, ever on the look-out for plants which will add something to their culinary enjoyment, who introduced us to it, for its culinary virtues were discovered by their King Henri IV.

In Lincolnshire, at one time the plant grew in every cottage garden, the young shoots in spring being simmered and served with melted butter; whilst in summer the leaves were cooked and used like curly kale. It is perennial, grows 2 ft. tall and is readily raised from seed sown in April.

Bush tomatoes may be grown in the food border, starting them off in May under barn cloches. Each plant should have about 2 sq. ft. of space so plant them here and there between other plants, but not where they will be shaded. Tiny Tim and Sleaford Abundance, both of which grow 15 in. tall, are suitable, their numerous small red fruits bringing a splash of brilliance to a border as they ripen. The Golden counterpart of Unwin's famous tomato, The Amateur is equally colourful.

Ruby chard, a variety of Swiss chard, will also add colour with its crimson stems like those of rhubarb and its large crinkled leaves. The stems grow 15 in. tall, the crimson extending through the veins of the leaves. The leaves may be cooked and served as spinach and have a less 'earthy' flavour, whilst being rich in vitamin content. The stems are pulled exactly as for rhubarb; cutting them will cause 'bleeding', for the plant is of the beet family. They should be removed before becoming too large and coarse. When young, simmer like asparagus and serve with meats or melted butter. If a sowing is made in early April, the sticks and leaves will be ready to use early in autumn, whilst a sowing made about 1 July will be ready to use the following spring. This later sowing must be confined to gardens south of the Trent.

New Zealand spinach is one of those plants which never look out of place in a border. Botanically it has nothing to do with spinach and is distinct in its habit, forming a low spreading plant and producing an abundance of thick fleshy leaves. Unlike spinach, it is quite untroubled by warm dry weather, whilst the leaves and tips of the young shoots may be picked over from early spring until Christmas. Sow seed in April where it is to grow (at the front of the border) and thin to 12 in. apart.

As with all vegetables, grow enough plants to give sufficient leaves for a cooking to serve two or four people, so depending upon the number in the house, allow at least four plants per person in order that there will always be a worthwhile picking. Most roots and garden peas are not really suitable for border planting, although sowings of radishes may be made in small circular groups anywhere space is available to the front, and similar sowings may be made of carrots and beetroot.

Greens such as the sprouting broccoli (the green sprouting calabrese being especially attractive) and brussels sprouts to bear a crop at various times of autumn and winter, will in no way appear out of place. Allow each plant about 1 sq. ft. to develop and make a sowing in April in a seed bed or in boxes, transplanting to the border when large enough to handle. These plants grow up to 2 ft. tall, so plant in groups of three or four and they will hold each other up during windy weather. They grow upright rather than spreading, forming their sprouts and shoots at the leaf joints, and they will crop for about six months. No garden should be without them. With its jade green foliage and shoots, the calabrese is a handsome plant. So, too, is the borecole or curly kale with its bright green crinkled leaves. From an April sowing it will be ready to gather from 1 September and throughout winter and spring. No plant possesses greater hardiness, hence it was once to be found in every north country garden, for the leaves become crisper after frost. But keep the plants picked over so that the leaves are always young and succulent.

Dwarf or French beans should have a place in the border, planting the seeds in late spring in groups of five or six for it is surprising how many beans a few plants will yield during the season. Masterpiece will do well in all types of soil and in all parts of Britain. Plant the seed 2 in. deep.

The most compact cabbages such as Primo and Greyhound could also be planted, setting out the plants wherever there is space and allowing each 1 sq. ft. to mature. Cut them before they grow too large and when they are sweet and succulent and in no way tough. Lettuce, too, should have a place and, here again, plant the more compact kinds such as Sugar Cos and Continuity. In more sheltered gardens, make a July sowing of All the Year Round to stand through winter.

The green curled endive is also suitable for border planting, for it is happy in the partial shade of other plants. It enjoys cool conditions and a moist humus-laden soil. Seed is sown mid-July, for the plants soon run to seed if sown earlier. Thin to 6 in. apart and begin using the leaves in salads from early October. They are crisper if blanched, so about ten days before required, draw the outer leaves over the heart and tie them with raffia and the heart

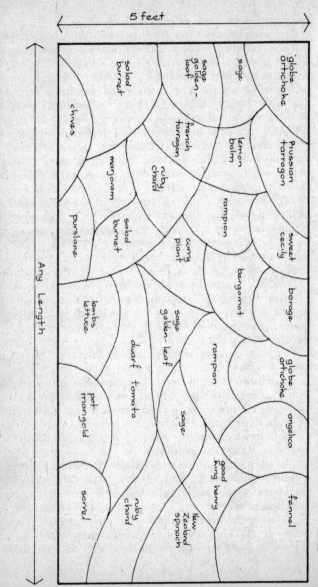

5 feet

Any Length

A border of food plants.

will soon blanch to a pale yellow colour.

To edge the border sow parsley which should be used in quantity, to garnish fish and most meat dishes, to sprinkle over vegetables, and to make parsley sauce to serve with steamed fish. It is so packed with health-giving salts and vitamins that it should be used with all savoury dishes. It will also make an invigorating drink if put through the juicer. Do not let the plants set seed and as soon as the flower stems appear, remove them, for it is the crisp curled leaves that are required, and the plants will make more leaf if not allowed to flower. Remember to sow fresh seed or it will take too long to germinate and old seed may never do so.

CHAPTER SIX

THE KITCHEN GARDEN

Where there is space, usually a plot at the end of the garden attached to many suburban town houses, a small part of it should be used for those vegetables which cannot be grown elsewhere. It may be desirable to concentrate them together, divided from the rest of the garden by a lattice or rustic pole fence covered with Oregon thornless blackberries to hide the unsightly stems of cabbages and sprouts.

A good spade, preferably of stainless steel, and a garden fork will be necessary for the preparation of the ground and they should be selected as the professional cricketer chooses his bats, to get the right 'feel', the correct balance and weight, for all people are of different sizes and shapes and it is necessary to make the task of digging as easy as possible. A rake for making the drills for seed sowing and to bring the surface to a fine tilth; a hoe to stir up the soil between the rows of plants and seeds and to suppress weeds; and a trowel for planting will be other necessary tools. A watering-can and hose will be needed at planting time and to keep the crops growing in summer. The tools should be cleaned after use, preferably wiping them with an oily rag so that when using them again, soil particles will not stick to them and make their use more laborious than necessary. Spend as much as you can afford on the tools for the better the quality, the easier the work, and good tools well looked after should last a lifetime.

CORRECTING SOIL DEFICIENCIES

If soil can be prepared in autumn this is the most suitable time, so that it will be ready for spring planting, but it may be made ready at any time from autumn until spring, whenever it is in an easily worked condition. Only clean, well-drained land with good humus content will produce healthy crops. A neglected town garden will rarely grow good vegetables unless the soil is first corrected for acidity, which will have come about with the accumulation of soot and sulphur deposits through the years. Give the soil a liberal dressing of hydrated lime, best done in autumn before turning over the soil, and give the surface a further dressing in early spring, though not where potatoes are being planted, for too much lime encourages scab. If possible, ask your local Horticultural Advisory Officer to test a sample of the soil for acidity and he will then say exactly how much lime is needed. For each hydrogen ion degree of acidity, the soil should be given a seven pound dressing of lime for every 1000 sq. ft. of ground. To grow most vegetables well, the soil should have a reaction of seven to eight, i.e. be slightly more alkaline than neutral (seven).

In addition to correcting acidity, lime enables the soil to release the various plant foods which may have been stored up over the years in neglected soils. If lime is absent, the crops cannot make use of these foods. Heavy land will benefit from a dressing with unhydrated or caustic lime which, when in contact with moisture in the soil, disintegrates by its explosive reaction and at the same time causes the soil to break up. If the ground can be roughly dug over in autumn and the caustic lime (obtainable from a builders' merchant) applied then, its action together with that of the rains and winds of winter will leave the soil in a friable, workable condition by early spring.

It is also possible to test soil for nitrogen, phosphorus and potash deficiency so that it may be corrected with the minimum of expense, for fertilizers are costly and must be used as economically as soil conditions will allow. The Horticultural Officer will test for these deficiencies too. To correct for nitrogen, apply a four ounce per sq. ft. dressing of sulphate of ammonia for each one per cent deficiency. For a one per cent phosphorus deficiency, dress the soil with four ounces of superphosphate of lime for every 100 sq. ft. of ground; and for a one per cent potash deficiency, rake in at planting time one ounce of sulphate of potash to every 100 sq. ft. of ground. All these are artificial or inorganic fertilizers; if some farmyard manure or composted straw (see section on mushrooms) can be dug into the ground when it is prepared, together with a liberal amount of bonfire ash, the quantities of artificials can be reduced by half.

Both heavy and light soils require humus as much as they do plant food. Humus will aerate a heavy soil to enable the bacteria to convert food into a form that can be best utilized by the plants, whilst a light sandy soil must have humus to make it retain moisture in summer. This is the time when most plant growth takes place and vegetables are composed of a large part of water. A good supply of moisture keeps them succulent and improves their eating quality in addition to promoting their rapid growth. A slowly grown vegetable will be hard and woody and devoid of flavour.

Farmyard manure, containing all the essential plant foods, is the best of all forms of humus but is now in short supply since farmers themselves are having to use all they can get. Cow manure is of special value for it quickly breaks down in the soil, whilst old mushroom bed compost is equally useful. Those who grow mushrooms themselves will find the original cost of their compost much reduced if it is also used to grow vegetables, although old mushroom compost is also readily obtainable from commercial mushroom establishments. Besides adding plant foods, it will open up a heavy soil and help to bind a sandy soil.

Another excellent form of humus is peat. With its slightly acid reaction this is particularly valuable to neutralize a calcareous soil which is usually a thin, hot soil, requiring plenty of humus to bring it into suitable condition for growing vegetables. Peat can be added as the ground is made clean in autumn or at any time, using it as a summer mulch for bush tomatoes and marrows and digging it into the soil as it is made ready for the various crops. Sphagnum moss peat is pale brown and as it is only partly decomposed, is able to retain the maximum amount of moisture, holding twenty times its own weight. A fourteen bushel bale, when shaken out, will cover 200 sq. ft. of ground to the depth of an inch. It is the best of all forms of humus for light land.

Hop manure and used brewer's hops, usually given for the asking, are also valuable forms of humus and plant food, whilst north country folk will be able to obtain for a small sum bags of cotton and wool waste known as shoddy. It contains nitrogen which, like farmyard manure, it releases slowly.

Those who live near the sea can gather seaweed from the beach in winter; when chopped with a sharp spade, it will soon break down in the soil and contains nitrogen and potash. Fish waste and fish meal, a quick-acting fertilizer containing all the plant foods, may also be obtainable.

Poultry manure is also a quick-acting and concentrated source of food and is best used when added to straw which is being composted with an activator, as described for mushroom compost. Garden compost from a bin which is made by driving stakes into the ground and fastening corrugated sheeting to them on three sides is also most valuable. Save every bit of green stuff not suitable for the kitchen and add lawn mowings, leaves and tea leaves. Newspapers, now expensive to buy, can be made of further use once they have been read by cutting them up and wetting them before adding to the compost heap. They are a valuable source of humus. Clearings from ditches may also be used, in fact anything of an organic nature, all of which can be saved during summer to fork into the ground in winter. The prunings of roses, hard-wooded shrubs and fruit trees, and the haulm of tomatoes and potatoes should be burnt and the ash used on the vegetable garden. Bonfire ash, which is a source of potash, should be kept under cover, for its potash content is soon washed away by rains and it will then have little value apart from making a clay soil lighter.

'Green' manuring is another excellent way of providing the soil with humus. This is often done to increase the depth of top soil over a gravel bed or over limestone, which would otherwise be a 'hot' shallow soil which would never grow good vegetables. Rape seed, which is inexpensive and quickly forms a dense mat of green fibrous roots, is sown in spring and when 2 in. high is dug into the soil as deeply as possible. Further sowings can even be made between crops and dug in before the next crop is planted.

THE USE OF FERTILIZERS

It is not advisable to use artificial or inorganic fertilizers until the soil is well supplied with humus. They provide the plants with food in concentrated form, but a soil which is not in good heart cannot make full use of these concentrates. Sulphate of ammonia and nitrate of soda have a high nitrogen content and are quick-acting. They are used for broccoli and spring cabbage which may need a stimulant to start them growing again after a hard winter. Slower in their action but less destructive to the structure of the soil are dried blood and soot, organics with almost as high a nitrogen content.

Nitrogen will also release the pent-up potash in the soil which is required for a plant to grow 'hard', to enable it to survive a severe winter, whilst it also improves the eating quality of vegetables. Potash is present in wood ash, which should be saved and stored under cover, but sulphate of potash has a far higher potash content and if used sparingly is not detrimental to the soil.

Phosphates stimulate root action. A small quantity of superphosphate should be raked into a seed bed, but it should also be present in all soils where young plants are grown, for it helps them to get away to a good start and reach quick maturity.

Liquid manure in its many forms also acts as a valuable tonic for crops reaching maturity. It can be obtained in proprietary form as Liquinure or can be made by immersing a sack filled with manure (or poultry manure) in a dustbin filled with water. Leave it for a week and use in diluted form, if possible when the soil is moist after rain. It will greatly improve the quality of vegetables.

The table below shows the action and content of fertilizers.

Fertilizer	Action	Nitrogen	Phosphates	Potash
Basic slag	Slow	15%	—	—
Bone meal	Slow	5%	20%	—
Dried blood	Medium	10%	—	—
Farm manure	Slow	0.5%	0.25%	0.5%
Fish meal	Quick	10%	8%	7%
Guano	Quick	15%	10%	7%
Kainit	Slow	—	—	13%
Nitrate of Soda	Quick	16%	—	—
Nitro-chalk	Quick	16%	—	—

Fertilizer	Action	Nitrogen	Phosphates	Potash
Potassium nitrate	Quick	14%	—	40%
Poultry manure	Medium	3%	2%	6%
Rape meal	Slow	5%	2%	1%
Seaweed	Slow	5%	—	1.5%
Shoddy	Slow	12%	—	—
Sulphate of ammonia	Quick	20%	—	—
Sulphate of potash	Quick	—	—	50%
Superphosphate	Medium	—	15%	—
Used hops	Slow	4%	2%	—

PREPARATION OF THE GROUND

To clean the ground of perennial weeds and to turn up the lower soil, which in town gardens is often of better quality than the surface soil, double digging is done. Take out a trench 12 in. deep at one end of the ground, moving the soil to the opposite end of the piece of land to be prepared, for it will be needed there to fill in the last trench. The humus is spread over the ground after removing the larger perennial weeds and this is incorporated into the next spit (the depth of a spade) of soil as it is turned into the trench. In this way the work proceeds until the last trench is filled in with the soil removed from the first spit. If the ground is of a heavy nature and not well drained, incorporate crushed brick, shingle or bonfire ash as the work proceeds. Shingle is obtained from a builders' merchant, or it may be collected from ditches or a gravel pit. The preparation of the ground at this stage should be done thoroughly, for afterwards it will be necessary only to dig over the top 6 in. and to add any fertilizers at that time. Sulphate of potash is usually given at planting time as it is quickly washed down into the soil and if given too soon much of its value will be lost to the plants.

If the digging is done in autumn or the early winter months and the surface left rough, the frosts and winter winds will pulverize the soil so that in spring it may be raked to a fine tilth.

Whilst preparing the soil, work in a wireworm exterminator for this can be a serious pest in town gardens. Gamma-BHC is highly effective but should not be used if potatoes are to be planted within twelve months. Bear in mind that potatoes are most useful in cleaning 'dirty' land, and it may be advisable to plant either the whole of the ground, or at least part of it, with nothing else in the first year.

CROP ROTATION

When the ground is in good order, thought must be given to rotational cropping. Moving the crops around each year will not only prevent the soil becoming 'sick' with any crop planted in the same soil year after year, but will also mean that the maximum use is obtained from the various fertilizers. For example, winter 'greens' take a large amount of nitrogen from the soil whilst the legumes (peas and beans) will leave the soil richer in nitrogen than before they were grown. For this reason, 'greens' should follow legumes and legumes follow roots, with potatoes also finding a place in the four-course rotation of crops for they will keep the ground clean. Moving the crops around each year will also keep the soil free from an accumulation of pests which are often endemic to one group of plants.

The most economical use of the ground will be obtained by taking as many crops off it in a year as climate allows. Those living in the south will be able to take three crops from parts of the vegetable garden: after cutting spring cabbage, sow French beans and follow with a quick-maturing autumn cauliflower or a crop of autumn lettuce. Those gardening south of the Trent will take only two crops off the same ground, and those north of the Trent will usually obtain but one crop unless the garden is sheltered and facing south. But inter-cropping may be done to increase the yield of the garden, planting quick-maturing salad crops between Brussels sprouts and winter cabbages, also between rows of French beans, the salads being cleared before the main crop plants reach maturity.

Cloches can also be used to bring on the salads, or to cover rows of quick-growing carrot or turnip sown between the slower-growing and later-maturing maincrop varieties for storing through winter. Or plant dwarf beans under cloches between rows of sprouts and savoys which will mature in winter. Trial and error will play a part in the cropping programme and it is surprising how much better (or worse) certain plants grow in one part of the country than another, however carefully the soil is prepared.

THE SEED BED

There should be a small seed bed in which to raise plants. Work some peat into the surface, which should be brought to a fine tilth before sowing. This is done in March, or early April in the north, the seed being sown in drills made 1 in. deep with the back of a rake. Make the drills from north to south, just as one does where sowing peas and beans, for then the plants will receive the light of the sun for most of the day whenever it shines. Early sowings of those plants requiring a long season to mature, e.g. celery and celeriac, are made in a propagator or frame, but sowings may also be made under cloches early in March. At this time a number of other plants may be raised under cloches to mature early.

Vegetable	Planting distance	To mature
Beetroot, Early Bunch	—	June-July
Cabbage, May Star	12 in.	May-June
Cabbage, Primo	12 in.	Early July
Carrot, Amsterdam Forcing	—	June-July
Carrot, Early Nantes	—	June-July
Carrot, Parisian Rondo	—	June-July
Cauliflower, Alpha	15 in.	July-August
Cauliflower, Snowball	12 in.	June-July
Lettuce, Little Gem	6 in.	June
Lettuce, Tom Thumb	6 in.	June
Spinach, Sigmaleaf	10 in.	July

Sow carrots and beetroot in drills 6 in. apart where they are to mature, thinning to 2 in. apart. The thinnings may be used immediately whilst the later roots should be pulled when about golf ball size, as with carrot Parisian Rondo and beet Early Bunch. A further sowing is made late in April and again towards the end of May to use in the same way, the maincrop varieties being kept for winter use. The culture of vegetables under cloches and frames is described elsewhere, but cloches may also be used for starting off the early crops, for then they will mature early in summer at a time when vegetables are scarce. An all-year-round supply of vegetables should be the aim of every gardener.

Where sowing in drills, use fresh seed and sow thinly so that the seedlings grow sturdy from the beginning. It is also important to transplant them before they become too big, as if they have been allowed to form a tap root they will take longer to re-establish themselves. If possible, move the plants during showery weather or failing this, give them plenty of water until established.

Always purchase seed from a reputable merchant who will guarantee almost one hundred per cent germination and a reliable strain, true to type. The price of top quality seed is still low in comparison with the cost of vegetables purchased from a greengrocer or in packets from the deep freezer of a supermarket. Pelleted seed saves much labour in thinning and enables the seeds to be spaced out correctly so that there is no loss through over-crowding. Pelleted seeds are dried to a low moisture level which causes the inert clay coating to break down quickly when in contact with moisture in the soil. The seed should be sown only just beneath the soil surface and lightly covered. It is possible to sow pelleted seed where the plants are to mature, thus removing the necessity for transplanting, but often it is not convenient to sow in this manner for the ground may be occupied by other crops reaching maturity.

It is important not to sow coated seed in over-wet soil for the coating tends to absorb more moisture than the seed requires for its germination, and in a too wet soil the coating will become a sludgy mass and may cause the seed to die through lack of air. Always sow when the soil is drying out after the winter rains, but before it becomes too dry. It is advisable not to sow pelleted seed in a heavy clay soil unless steps have been taken to drain it.

GROWING-ON THE PLANTS

When transplanting, set the plants well into the soil to prevent them from being blown over by winter winds as they grow heavier. Earthing up whilst they are growing will also help to prevent this. When lifting the young plants from the rows, place them in a shallow bowl with their roots in water and after planting, make firm. This will help them form a solid head, or tight sprouts in the case of Brussels sprouts. After planting, keep the hoe moving between the plants or between the rows, as for root crops. This will stir the soil and stop it panning or setting hard on top, preventing water from reaching the roots and depriving the bacteria in the soil of much-needed oxygen. Hoeing will also kill annual weeds which otherwise would choke the young vegetable plants before they can re-establish themselves.

Always water in the evening, which will allow the moisture to reach down to the roots of the plants without a hot sun drying it up before it does so, and always give sufficient water for the plants to have a thorough soaking, otherwise they will turn up their roots to the surface in search of it.

During dry weather, both dwarf and runner beans will benefit from a daily syringing of the flowers and foliage. This will help the flowers to set and keep the plants free from red spider. It will also keep the plants fresh, but beans also require copious amounts of water at the roots to produce those succulent stringless pods which are so appreciated. Melons and marrows, too, require ample supplies of moisture, and if root crops are deprived they will be coarse and woody when cooked. Attention to watering is a most important aspect of an efficiently run vegetable garden.

The correct time to harvest and store vegetables is described under the appropriate varieties in the following pages.

A Selection of Vegetables for the Garden

ARTICHOKE, GLOBE
See Chapter 5: 'Food from the Border'

ARTICHOKE, JERUSALEM
This differs from the globe artichoke in that it grows under the soil, the tubers being tasty and nourishing, but it is neglected by modern gardeners for their knobbly skin is difficult to clean.

Dig some humus-forming manure into the soil — old mushroom bed compost is ideal — and give the ground a dusting of superphosphate at planting time. Like shallots, the tubers should be planted before the end of March, these being the first vegetables to plant, along with the Windsor varieties of the broad bean. Plant small tubers about walnut size, in V-shaped drills made 5-6 in. deep, allowing 15 in. between the tubers in the rows and 2 ft. between the rows. Earthing up the rows early in May will increase the yield. Lift the roots towards the end of October as the tops die down and store in boxes of sand, or begin lifting mid-September as required and lift the others late in October to store for winter use.

ASPARAGUS

This is found in few gardens today, for it takes several years before any worthwhile cuttings can be made. Yet it is a food for epicures and should be grown wherever possible. However, as the bed will remain undisturbed for years, the soil must be well prepared.

It is a maritime plant, requiring a well-drained sandy soil, so make a raised bed 6 in. above the surrounding ground at one end of the vegetable garden. If the bed is made 6 ft. wide, this will allow for three rows with almost 3 ft. between each; plant the same distance apart in the rows. Trenches are made 9 in. deep and plenty of humus is placed at the bottom then covered with 3 in. of soil into which has been incorporated a two ounce per sq. yd. dressing of superphosphate and one ounce per sq. yd. of sulphate of potash.

Then spread out the spider-like roots over a small mound of soil and fill in the trench. Do not expose the roots to the drying winds prevalent in late March, which is the best planting time. Salad crops can be grown between the rows for the first two years.

No sticks should be removed the first year. Allow them to form plenty of fern but do not let them seed. Remove the flowers and cut the foliage almost to ground level when it turns brown in autumn. Then give the plants a dressing with salt.

Next year, a few sticks can be cut (with a sharp knife) from each plant, and more each year, but always leave some to make fern and so maintain the vigour of the roots.

Two excellent varieties are the American Connover's Colossal and Early Argenteuil from France. Both bear large sticks of excellent flavour, the latter being ready two weeks earlier, thus spreading the season.

BEAN, BROAD

Broad beans like a soil which has been well manured for a previous crop. If not, work in a quantity of decayed manure, particularly like old mushroom-bed compost. A double row may be sown early November and left unprotected through winter, but at this time do not sow the Windsor varieties for they are less hardy. Make the rows 9 in. apart and allow the same distance between the beans in the rows. Black fly will rarely trouble autumn sown plants. Plant the seeds 2 in. deep. A second sowing of the Windsor varieties should be made in March, to mature when the earlier crop is reaching its end. Where the soil is heavy, only a spring sowing should be made.

Most varieties will require supporting. This is done as the plants make growth in spring by placing stout stakes at regular intervals along the rows, to which twine is fastened when the plants are 12 in. above soil level. Add another row of twine when the plants reach a height of 2 ft. Additional support can be given by drawing up the soil to the plants all along the rows which is done early in May.

VARIETIES

Dreamlight, which received an Award of Merit at the R.H.S. Trials in 1966, is both a heavy bearer and has outstanding flavour, each pod containing eight or nine beans (seeds).

The Sutton. It is hardy for autumn planting and as it grows only 12 in. tall is suitable for an exposed garden. It matures early, the seeds being white.

Unwin's Longfellow is hardy and does well in all soils, the freely produced pods containing eight or nine beans.

PESTS

Black Fly. It is the real menace with the broad bean but may be controlled by pinching out the tops of the plants as soon as a fair crop has set. This discourages the fly and also makes for early maturity. Early in May, spray the plants once a week with liquid derris which will also keep the pest under control. Another tip is to sow a row of summer savory near to the beans and this will keep them free from the pest.

BEAN, FRENCH OR DWARF

For a succession of beans from early summer until late autumn, make several sowings over a period of three to four months, the first under barn-type cloches in early April or in the most favourable districts, early March. Use an early maturing variety like Sutton's Premier in northern gardens early in May in the open, for the plants will not appear until risk of frost has departed. In the south, make a sowing outdoors early April. Another sowing should follow at the end of June or early in July, using a quick-maturing variety.

For an early crop where no cloches are available, it will be possible to make a sowing in a sunny bed, between lettuce or spring cabbages. The seed is sown about 1 May and, if late frosts are not experienced, an early crop will be obtained. It is a risk worth taking.

Dwarf beans present no difficulties with their culture. They like a rich soil, one containing nitrogen and humus, preferably given as decayed manure which is deeply dug into the ground during winter. French beans generally follow a crop of lettuce or late-maturing broccoli, for which the ground has been well manured in autumn. If this is so, no further manure will be necessary but a half ounce per sq. yd. dressing of superphosphate and the same of potash raked in just before planting time will increase the yield. Four ounces of seed will sow a 40 ft. row which should give twenty pounds of beans.

If sowing under cloches, sow a double row, spacing the seeds 6 in. apart in the rows. To allow for any misses, it is advisable to sow two seeds together, removing one if two seeds germinate or sow a dozen seeds under the end cloche. Or if sowing late in April rather than early in the month, space the seed 3 in. apart and move alternate plants to the open ground about mid-May. This is a more satisfactory method than sowing directly into the open where slugs prove troublesome in a damp season. Alternatively, seed may be sown in deep boxes in a cold frame, or directly into the frame in a friable compost, sowing early in May after the vegetable plants have been hardened off. The young beans are set out into the open 6 in. apart at the end of May after hardening. The plants will require no further attention, but keep the hoe moving between the rows and water regularly in dry weather. Beans are copious drinkers. Remove the beans as soon as they reach a reasonable size, when they are fresh and succulent. If allowed to remain on the plants too long they will become tough and stringy. They mature quickly and from the end of July until late September it is advisable to look over the plants daily.

VARIETIES

Canadian Wonder is an old favourite and still outstanding for planting under cloches, and *Sutton's Premier* is also excellent. For early crops outdoors plant *Masterpiece,* bearing multitudes of long straight pods of darkest green. It is the best all-purpose variety ever introduced. *Earligreen* is also excellent for early crops, the pods measuring up to 6 in. long; also *Limelight* from Thompson & Morgan. For maincrop, *The Prince* matures quickly in all soils, the thick, fleshy pods reaching 9 in. without becoming stringy. A four ounce packet of seed will sow a 50 ft. row.

BEAN, HARICOT

These are grown for their beans, which are dried. First allow the pods to hang until the end of summer for the beans to become quite hard. If the pods have to be gathered before they are fully ripe, spread them out in a dry, sunny room to complete their ripening. The beans will then remove easily from the pods. Store them in a clean cardboard box as tins tend to sweat and the beans will then deteriorate. It is the white and pale-coloured seeded varieties that should be used for drying; those with black and brown seeds being used only for sauces.

Comtesse de Chambord is the best variety for drying; although the seed is small in comparison with others, the skin is thin, the flavour excellent. Owing to the small size of the seed, only a quarter of a pound is required to sow a 15 yd. row.

Dried haricot beans should be soaked in water for upwards of two hours before cooking.

BEANS, RUNNER OR CLIMBING

Runner beans come later into bearing, and may even be classed as a late-summer and autumn crop. They are valuable for prolonging the summer vegetable season. They require staking, and since a matured crop is heavy and has to withstand winds in the autumn, the scarlet runner requires more attention than the climbing French bean.

The runner bean is less hardy than the dwarf bean, and so must not be sown until early May in the south; at the end of the month in the north.

The plants make plenty of foliage and crop heavily. They are also gross feeders, and so the ground should be trenched. Where the beans are to be planted, remove about 12 in. of soil and into the bottom of the trench put garden refuse or compost such as decayed cabbage and broccoli leaves. Over this, place a layer of soil and a little decayed manure. The trench is filled up during the winter months and is then allowed to settle down before it is topped up with soil to which is added half an ounce of superphosphate and half an ounce of potash per yard of trench.

Erect the stakes before sowing the seed. Fish netting is suitable if neither canes nor wood laths are available, but whatever is used it must be made strong enough to hold a heavy weight of foliage. Stout poles should be deeply inserted into the ground at intervals of 8 ft. and they and the laths are held together by fastening them to strong galvanized wire.

The seed is planted with a trowel on either side of the netting and spaced 8 in apart in the row; or plant one seed to each lath or cane. After planting, a number of seeds should be sown in a frame, or in a small seed bed, to transplant if there are any misses in the row.

When the plants begin to form their first beans, feed with manure water each week, if possible given during a rainy period. Early in August, the plants will benefit from a mulch of strawy manure.

Scarlet runner beans are the most copious drinkers of all vegetables and must not be allowed to suffer from lack of moisture at the roots or the beans will grow tough and stringy, whilst regular spraying of the foliage will help the flowers to set, and will keep the plants fresh and free from red spider. When watering the roots, give a thorough soaking before syringing the foliage and flowers.

VARIETIES

Crusader, a recent introduction, is outstanding for a dry summer for it does not easily drop its flowers through lack of moisture. The pods grow large and fleshy but in no way coarse. *Streamline* is best for a heavy soil, its long narrow pods reaching 18 in. and are of excellent flavour; whilst Dobies' *Yardstick* though reaching a great size is succulent and stringless and of delicious flavour. The new variety *Desirée* bears stringless pods and few seeds so that the pods are very fleshy.

BEAN, VEGETABLE

This was introduced into commerce by a Swedish agriculturist and is known as Fiskeby V, being the above-ground counterpart of the soya bean. It is a wonder food, containing more than twenty times the nutritious protein value of any other vegetable, half a cup of beans (about one hundred) containing the same protein as a quarter pound of steak. Raw tomatoes contain one per cent protein, the vegetable bean forty per cent, whilst it has ten times the potassium content of fresh milk and contains almost as much calcium.

The bean requires a warm summer to crop well, when up to fifty pods can be expected from a single plant. Where sweet corn grows well, so will this crop. To allow it more time to mature, seed is sown in small pots, one to each, under glass about mid-April for planting out mid-May in the south after hardening, or at the end of the month in the north, for these plants are not frost hardy; or sow under cloches on 1 May. In the open, sow the seeds (which are like dwarf bean seeds) about 1 June, in rows 12 in. apart, planting the beans 1 in. deep and 6 in. apart in the rows. A soil in good 'heart' is all that is necessary, but line the drills with peat before sowing. Keep the soil well watered and pick the pods (as for dwarf beans) when the beans can be seen bulging in them, for it is the beans that are required, not the pods. To maintain a succession, make another sowing in early July. After shelling, steam until tender and serve with a little melted butter. They eat like roast chestnuts, being floury and with a similar flavour.

BEET, PERPETUAL

Perpetual beet is also known as spinach beet, on account of the similarity of its top foliage to spinach when cooked. It is a root crop, but the root is not used, only the tops, which are able to withstand hard frost, and may be sown both in spring for summer use, and again at the beginning of July to use until Christmas. For it to produce an abundance of leaf, a soil rich in nitrogen should be provided. Dig in plenty of decayed manure, particularly shoddy if it can be obtained, or well composted straw, and sow the seed in drills 18 in. apart, thinning the plants to 9 in. in the rows. One ounce of seed will sow a 20 ft. row. The leaves, if gathered when young, possess a richer and less earthy flavour than spinach.

BEETROOT

A universal favourite which has lost none of its popularity over the years. For bottling, to preserve in malt vinegar, the new Non-Bleeding Beet should be used, for unlike the ordinary beets, it does not lose its crimson colour when sliced.

Beetroot is a maritime plant, preferring a sandy soil, and some salt in its diet. Dress the ground with one ounce per sq. yd. of common salt before sowing. At the same time, rake in half an ounce of superphosphate and the same of sulphate of potash and give no other manures if the soil was manured for a previous crop and is in a friable condition.

As it is not quite hardy beetroot must not be sown until mid-April in the south, early May in the north. Sow in drills 1 in. deep and 15 in. apart and thin out the plants to 6 in. in the rows. An ounce of seed will sow a 20 yd. row.

Never allow the plants to lack moisture or the roots will grow coarse and bitter whilst the plants may run to seed long before they mature. To conserve moisture, give a peat mulch between the rows early in July.

The roots may be used as they reach tennis-ball size for summer salads and with meats when boiled or having first been pickled in vinegar. If a second sowing is made early in June, to mature in autumn, they may be pickled as lifted, or stored in boxes of dry sand in a frost free room for using in salads and for pickling through winter as required.

When lifting beet do so with care for the smallest cut will cause most varieties to bleed. Before storing or before the freshly-lifted roots are boiled, twist off the leaves rather than cut off with a knife; only twisting will prevent bleeding.

VARIETIES

Boltardy. It forms a large globe of crimson-red and does not easily run to seed in dry weather but the older *Detroit Globe* is still unsurpassed for quality, being free of 'rings' when cooked and pickled. *Cheltenham Greentop* is a long-rooted beet of exceptional flavour, and is sweet and succulent when used in salads. For pickling, the new *Non-Bleeding Beet* will not lose its crimson colour when cut and sliced.

BROCCOLI, LARGE-HEADED

If it is to come through a hard winter, broccoli must be well grown from the time the seed is sown. The plants are ready to harvest exactly twelve months after sowing so that those required for March should be sown the previous March and so on, a succession being sown until late May of varieties to mature from March until early June when early cauliflowers will take over.

It is particularly important with broccoli to obtain the best strains of seed, for the plants must not only withstand the winter but at the same time should have formed a large compact head. It is disappointing to have to wait a full year for the plant to reach maturity if in the end there is only a poor head to cut.

As they have to remain in the ground through winter, it means that the plants must be grown 'hard'; yet they must receive enough nitrogen to make a good sized head. This means a humus rich soil and one in which the manure releases its nitrogen slowly, over a long period. A soil heavily manured for a previous crop and to which has been added two ounces per sq. yd. of hoof or horn meal just previous to planting, will be suitable. The soil should also be given a one ounce per sq. yd. dressing with potash at planting time to help the plants withstand the winter. A firm seed bed is also necessary and give the plants plenty of room. They are set out 2 ft. apart each way.

The way the plants are raised is just as important as the preparation of the land. To withstand the winter, short sturdy plants are necessary. Sow the seed thinly and thin the plants if they are too close. If the plants are 'drawn' and 'leggy', they will not recover. One ounce of seed will produce more than a hundred plants.

Where seed is sown over a hot bed, it may be necessary to transplant into a cold frame, otherwise the plants may make too much growth and become 'drawn' before they are planted out.

VARIETIES

The first to mature is Sutton's *Safeguard Protecting*, which is ready by early March, the heads in no way troubled by a severe winter. To follow in April and May, *Leamington* is recommended. Then comes Dobies' *Royal Oak* which makes a compact plant for a small garden, the pure white heads being ready to cut in June and the latest of all is Methuen's *June*, which in the north is not ready until early July.

BROCCOLI, SPROUTING

In cold, exposed districts this vegetable, with the Brussels sprout, should be first choice. With sprouts, it is also the most economic. As all varieties of sprouting broccoli will occupy the ground for a long season, several continuing to bear their shoots for two years, they must be given a rich soil, in which the nitrogen content is slowly released. Clean ground and a soil similar to that prepared for the cauliflower-headed broccoli will be suitable. It is also advisable to give the plants a mulch of strawy manure in early winter and this is forked into the ground early in spring but do not work too close to the plants.

As sprouting broccoli will grow tall, a sheltered place should be chosen, where the plants will not be blown over by strong winds early in spring. Plant firmly and ensure that during winter, the plants are made firm after frost and wind.

Sow in April and thinly, so that the plants do not become 'drawn' in the rows. Plant out 2 ft. apart early May, and keep the soil hoed in summer. The first shoots will be ready for using from early the following March, though the Calabrese will be ready in the autumn after sowing. The shoots are cooked whole, braised and served with sauce – either mushroom or cheese sauce being a happy combination.

The shoots or sprouts (not to be confused with Brussels sprouts), should be removed when young and tender for they will quickly run to seed if left ungathered, especially with the warmer weather of late spring.

VARIETIES

Early Purple Sprouting. Sow early April, and it will be ready for using early the following spring.

Late Purple Sprouting. Coming into use late in April, it will continue to bear a profusion of richly-flavoured shoots up to July, when peas and beans demand our attention.

Nine-Star Perennial. It is truly perennial in a rich soil, and if given a regular mulch in spring each year, it will bear its pure white shoots, like tiny cauliflowers, for up to five years; during spring and early summer producing nine or ten heads from every plant. For exposed gardens it should be grown where late broccoli or early cauliflowers often fail. It grows tall and should be planted against a fence, or in an out-of-the-way part of the garden where it can be left undisturbed for years. If the sprouts come in quantity, remember that they freeze well.

BRUSSELS SPROUTS

The most important of winter 'greens' on account of its desirable eating qualities and its long season of production. Hard tight sprouts of walnut size are wanted in the kitchen when there will be little waste, and they are obtained only by planting in a compact soil. Also, the plants will not bear heavily unless in a rich soil.

Brussels sprouts occupy the ground for a long period, eighteen months from the time the seed is sown until the plants are removed, during which time they produce upwards of fifty sprouts per plant. They require a soil in which nitrogen is slowly released over a long period. The ground should be prepared in winter, digging in plenty of garden compost or farmyard manure, and giving the soil a generous application of lime. In early spring four ounces per sq. yd. of hoof or horn meal should be forked in. This will release its nitrogen during the entire life of the crop. An excess of nitrogenous artificials will cause the sprouts to grow loose and coarse. Soot, raked into the soil before planting, is valuable for it will also release its nitrogen content over a long period. In addition, the soil should be given one ounce per sq. yd. dressing of superphosphate and potash at lanting time. Firm planting is essential, and to prevent the rather tall, heavy plants from being blown about, tread round each plant regularly during winter and after strong winds.

This attention to detail might be considered excessive, but cropping is heavy from October until April, with almost daily gathering of sprouts, yielding between one and two pounds per plant. If there are too many to use, they freeze well.

Sprouts take a long time to grow and to crop so make two

sowings, one in late August to come into bearing early the following autumn; another in March, or if a frame is available, sow in February, to begin bearing late autumn when those sown earlier are coming to an end. By also sowing a late variety, the plants will begin to crop at Christmas and continue until April. Sow thinly so that transplanting at the seedling stage is not necessary and when large enough the plants are set out 2 ft. apart.

Sprouts, like so many winter greens, are at their best following light frost. This makes them crisp and brings out their flavour, and they should be gathered just before being used. Keep the plants free of decayed leaves as they turn yellow.

VARIETIES

If only one variety can be grown, then let it be *Peer Gynt*, an F1 Hybrid which makes a dwarf, compact plant, packed from top to bottom with medium-sized tight sprouts of delicious flavour. They are ready from 1 October and continue until January. The older *Aristocrat* is also a reliable variety, forming its sprouts over a long season, whilst to mature from January until April the new variety *Citadel* is outstanding, the sprouts being uniform and darkest green with a distinctive flavour. *Achilles* is another of good flavour and bears over the whole of winter if grown well.

CABBAGE, SPRING

This is one of the most important of vegetables, for the crop may be cut during those sparse late-spring and early-autumn months when, apart from the sprouting broccoli, there is little else available. The plants never attain the large size of autumn and winter cabbages, so never become coarse and strongly flavoured. They are also admirable for a small garden.

With spring cabbage, timing is all important for they have to be strong enough to withstand the winter weather, yet must not be grown too quickly, when they grow 'soft' and may be damaged by frost. Again, if they are too advanced, there is a tendency for them to 'bolt' (run to seed) if the spring is dry and warm.

In the south, where plant growth continues until November, make a sowing early in August; in the north, a month earlier.

Sow thinly in a prepared seed bed and in shallow drills 9 in. apart. Keep free from weeds, and water if dry conditions prevail.

Set out the plants early September in the north, a month later in more favourable areas, the ground having been manured and supplied with humus, allowing it time to consolidate before planting. A two ounce per sq. yd. dressing with basic slag should be raked in at planting time. As spring cabbages never grow very large, they may be set out about 18 in. apart each way. Except for keeping the hoe moving between the rows, they will require no further attention, but give them a half ounce per sq. yd. dressing with nitrate of soda on a rainy day when growth commences in spring.

When ready, cut the heads rather than uproot the plants. From the place where the cut is made will appear a succession of succulent, small heads which may be steamed in butter and are very different from those large stringy winter cabbages boiled (and served) in water in most hotels.

PESTS AND DISEASES

Owing to the frequency of club root amongst members of the brassica family, 'greens' should be given fresh ground every year on a four-year rotation though the disease (which causes swelling of the roots) may be prevented by dipping the roots in calomel solution when transplanting. It will also prevent an attack of root fly.

Plants may also be damaged by caterpillars of the common cabbage white butterfly, especially in a dry summer when the creamy white grubs will penetrate to the centre of cauliflowers and sprouts, making them virtually unusable. To control, dust the plants with derris once every ten days from 1 June until 1 September.

VARIETIES

Emerald Cross. An F1 Hybrid, it forms ball-like heads of emerald green and shows great uniformity. Sow in succession to mature late summer and autumn.

Flower of Spring. It matures early and makes a good-sized plant, compact and pointed, and is of excellent flavour.

Greyhound. The first of the pointed cabbages to mature, this is a valuable variety to bridge the gap between the early spring and summer maturing cabbages. It is dwarf and compact, with few outer leaves.

Unwin's Foremost. A new variety rapidly becoming a favourite for its firm, dark-green heads and delicate, tender flavour. With its compact habit it is ideal for a small garden.

CABBAGE, AUTUMN

To continue the supplies when the spring cabbage finishes in June, there are cabbages which will make plants little larger than the spring varieties, and which for mildness and tender eating are superior to those that are grown for winter use. They may be said to come somewhere between the two in habit of growth, also in their season of maturing.

Seed is sown early September, the young plants remaining in the seed bed through winter. They should be protected, in cold parts, from frost by bracken or short twiggy sticks, or the drills may be covered with cloches. Or sow in March.

Early in April, the plants are set out exactly as for spring cabbage and will have formed small, well-hearted heads to mature August and September.

VARIETIES

Autumn Queen. It bridges the gap until the winter cabbages are ready in November and makes a small, ball-like head of good flavour.

Golden Acre. Like Primo, it is early to mature and makes a compact ball-shaped head which sits on the ground like a football.

Primo. It makes a dwarf, ball-like head of delicate flavour and tenderness, being an ideal cabbage for a small family.

CABBAGE, WINTER

By the end of the year the cabbage will give way to the savoy for, with its crinkled leaves which allow moisture to drain away, the savoy does not decay as do cabbages during prolonged rain. To mature November and December, sow early in April, and when planting out allow 18-20 in. in and between the rows, for winter cabbages make larger heads.

Town garden soils which tend to be of an acid nature should be given a two ounce per sq. yd. dressing of nitro-chalk before planting, after working in a liberal quantity of farmyard manure, or if in small amounts, augmented by hoof or horn meal, giving a handful per square yard. Like all brassicas, winter cabbages enjoy a soil containing plenty of nitrogen which is released slowly over several months.

VARIETIES

Enkhuizen Glory. A continental variety, making a large solid head which stands for a long time after it has hearted.

January King. It resembles a savoy in that the leaves are crinkled and fold over. It is the most frost-resistant of all cabbages, standing through January, but cooks soft and tender.

Winnigstadt. A fine cabbage for late autumn use, making solid, pointed hearts which do well in all soils.

Winter White. Sown early in April, it will produce enormous round heads for cutting late in November, when those heads not required for immediate use may be pulled up with the roots and stored in a shed or cellar for several weeks.

CABBAGE, CHINESE

It originates from China and the Far East and is a dual-purpose vegetable, the leaves being eaten in a salad up to Christmas as a substitute for lettuce; or they may be steamed in butter and served with meats. They are delicious either way, having a mild flavour.

The Chinese or Pe-tsai cabbage as it is called, is given the same treatment as the endive, a not-too-rich soil, but one containing some moisture-holding humus. Unlike ordinary cabbages, the plants readily run to seed, so do not sow until early July. Thin out the seedlings, those remaining being left where they are to mature for it does not transplant well. Keep the hoe moving between the rows, and water during dry periods.

The best variety is *Wong-Bok,* which is hardy, the leaves being crisp and tender, whilst it does not easily run to seed.

Making a larger head and growing taller is *Chihili,* the dark green leaves folding over like those of a large cos lettuce.

CABBAGE, RED

The secret of success with this cabbage is that it must be given a long growing season. Seed is sown early in September, and the plants remain in the rows through winter. In March, plant into a well-limed soil enriched with plenty of manure. Plant 2 ft. apart, making the plants quite firm. A one ounce per sq. yd. dressing each of superphosphate and sulphate of potash should be raked in at planting time. Through summer keep the hoe moving, and give a sprinkling of sulphate of ammonia around the plants during a rainy period at the end of April to stimulate them into growth. Cut the ball-like heads late in autumn.

VARIETIES

Early Blood Red. Deepest crimson when pickled, it is the best variety for northern gardens where the growing season is shorter than in the south, for it does not take so long to make a small, compact head.

Stockley's Giant. Makes a huge head, tender and sweet and of a rich, blood-red colour. It needs a long growing season and a well-manured soil.

CALABRESE

Also called Italian or Green Sprouting. Around a central green head, numerous small shoots continue to form from late summer until the end of the year and it should be used at this time, leaving the bulk of the Brussels sprouts until later for they will not be harmed by hard frosts, and the sprouting broccoli for late winter and spring.

The calabrese likes a humus-laden soil rich in nitrogen, which is slowly released over a long time, yet it is an accommodating vegetable which will grow almost anywhere, and crops well in a town garden, nor does it occupy the ground as long as the other sprouting broccoli.

Seed is sown in drills in the open, in late or early April. Sow thinly, allowing 9 in. between the drills, so that the hoe may be taken between. The plants are set out during April 18 ins. apart each way into a well-firmed soil. They require little attention, apart from keeping the ground free from weeds. A second sowing is made in May to extend the season until Christmas.

Early August the first heads will be ready for cutting, and will continue cropping until October, when those from a later sowing are ready. The side shoots will appear as fast as they can be cut, but if there are too many to use, they will freeze perfectly.

VARIETIES

Express Corona is the earliest to mature and develops a heavy crop of side shoots in early autumn. When steamed, the flavour is outstanding. For later crops plant *Autumn Spear,* which can be used until the end of the year. Cook it in bundles like asparagus.

CARROT

This likes a soil which has been manured for a previous crop, for in freshly manured ground, the roots grow forked. It is a valuable crop for sowing early over a hotbed or in a frame, as described in the chapter on frames. For the maincrop, sow in drills early in April. A fine seed bed is essential to obtain long, tapering roots. Keep the seedlings moist and thin to 2 in. apart, using the thinnings in the kitchen.

The only real pest is carrot fly, which troubles almost all root crops. The flies lay their eggs in the soil and the yellow larvae burrow into the roots, causing the plants to die. To prevent, dust the rows with Lindex at sowing time and again shortly after the seedlings appear.

VARIETIES

For an early main crop, *Chantenay Red Core,* a stump-rooted carrot, is of pleasing flavour and whose core is the same colour as the flesh. *Scarlet Perfection* is similar and is an excellent keeper; likewise *Sutton's Favourite* with its long stump root of exhibition quality. Also excellent for an early maincrop is Sutton's *Champion Scarlet Horn.*

The new *Juwarot* is remarkable for its richness in vitamin A, containing two hundred and fifty mg. per kilo when raw, or double that of others, whilst it is sweet and juicy in a salad or when steamed in butter.

CAULIFLOWER

One of the most difficult vegetables to grow well, to form a large compact head, cauliflowers must be grown in a soil not lacking moisture. They must therefore be given a soil rich in humus. Like all 'greens', they require an abundance of nitrogen, best given in the form of decayed farmyard manure, old mushroom-bed compost, wool shoddy, or compost prepared from straw, for besides supplying nitrogen, these manures will also provide humus.

The land must also be limed, and another requirement for compact heads is potash. This is given together with a dressing of superphosphate at planting time, at the rate of one ounce each per square yard. If the spring is cold and the plants are slow to grow away, dust around each a small quantity of nitrate of soda to stimulate them into growth. This is given in wet weather.

In dry weather, the plants should be watered at regular intervals, for otherwise the heads will be small, and will run to seed almost as quickly as they mature.

As the heads will not hold for long, it is advisable to plant for succession, rather than to make large-scale plantings. Make the first sowing in a frame in early March, and sow outdoors in April and May. Home users should commence cutting the heads the moment they become of reasonable size, otherwise those left until later may have passed their best. If you have too many to use fresh, this vegetable freezes admirably but choose the curds (heads) when at their best.

VARIETIES

Cambridge Early Allhead. A new variety which matures early from a spring sowing. Of dwarf, compact habit, the heads are of fine texture and should be used as soon as they mature.

Dwarf Monarch. The most compact late variety for a small garden, and forming a medium-sized head of exceptional quality. It is at its best in October from a May sowing.

Snow King. An F1 Hybrid, it is quick to mature, producing large solid white heads in three months after planting whilst it does not readily run to seed in dry weather.

Snowdrift. A second early to follow Early Allhead and bearing a large white head well-protected by its leaves. This variety stands well in hot weather without running to seed.

Veitch's Self-Protecting. The best winter cauliflower, the incurved leaves afford protection to the large, well-shaped heads until the end of the year, it being the hardiest of all varieties. In a

CELERY, SELF-BLANCHING

This requires different culture from the ordinary celery and is less demanding in its needs. It is grown in beds on the flat, rather than in trenches, in a soil enriched with some decayed manure or garden compost.

Seed is sown under glass in January, in a warm greenhouse or frame or over a hotbed and, after transplanting and hardening, the young plants are set out early in June 10-12 in. apart. Plant firmly and never allow them to suffer from lack of water. By 1 September, the first 'sticks' may be lifted and used as soon as possible afterwards. Used raw, grated in salads or stewed, this is a delicious vegetable with a more subtle flavour than the ordinary celery.

Golden Self-Blanching is the best variety, the heart being self-folding, pure white and tender. Where the 'sticks' are required for eating raw, they will be more succulent and sweeter if cardboard is tied around the stems for about three weeks before using. This takes only a few minutes, if the cardboard is cut beforehand. It is tied at the top and bottom of the stems with raffia, but no earthing is necessary.

CHICORY

See Chapter 9: 'Food from Dark Places'.

CRESS, AMERICAN LAND

This is an excellent substitute for watercress for it needs no water, and is not so much trouble to grow. It is perennial, and the best way to grow it is to make up a bed in a partially-shaded position, where the plants may be kept cool and shielded from the sun in summer. The bed should be divided into two parts, one for cutting in summer, the other for late autumn and winter use.

Seed is sown in March in a cold frame or under cloches in a soil containing plenty of humus. When large enough to handle, move the plants to a prepared bed, spacing them 8 in. apart and water in. The bed should have been deeply dug, and have had liberal quantities of well-decayed manure incorporated. Like all salad crops, land cress likes a well-nourished soil so that the shoots will be mild and succulent. The seed may also be sown in

sheltered place it may be left until January, to bridge
til the earliest broccoli is ready.

Those varieties which are not self-protecting and
to stand out from late autumn should have their heads
partially breaking and bending over the leaves. A hea
hard frost will turn brown and be of no use for cooki
ing.

CELERIAC

It is a root with the celery flavour and where cele
difficult to manage, celeriac should be grown inste
grows readily though needs a long season. Plants shoul
be raised in a warm greenhouse or over a gentle hotbe
spring, the seed being sown early March, keeping the fr
ed. The seed should be kept comfortably moist, when it
minate by the end of the month, and the seedlings be
transplanting to a cold frame or to boxes of compost
The young plants must never be allowed to lack mois
must be grown on steadily until time to plant out at th
May.

Celeriac is planted on the flat, there being nowhere
much labour attached to its culture as to that of celery. It
no blanching, no earthing up, nor so rich a soil but it doe
deeply-dug soil containing some humus such as peat and d
manure or garden compost. It enjoys best a friable loan

Set out the plants 1 ft. apart each way, with the
bulbous-like root just sittiland whenever the soil is dry, and
the soil away from the root which will grow half-out
ground. Towards the end of September, the soil is scraped
from the roots, and any shoots which grow out from their
removed with a sharp knife.

In the south the roots may be left in the ground all winter
used when required. In this way they will better retain
strong celery flavour and nuttiness. In the north they shoul
lifted late in November, the tops being removed and the r
trimmed. They will store through winter in boxes of sand in
shed or building. The best variety is Giant Prague which mak
large root, free of fibres.

early August and wintered in a frame, setting out the plants in spring.

If the soil is kept moist, the first shoots will be ready for cutting towards the end of summer. They are almost exactly like those of watercress, being of deep green and possessing a strong flavour.

To enjoy the green sprigs through winter, cover half the bed with a light (i.e. a sheet of glass), having first erected boards around the part to be covered. Admit plenty of air on all suitable days, but should the weather be severe, close up the frame and water only occasionally in winter. Remove the frame light early in spring.

CUCUMBER, RIDGE

Where neither frames nor cloches are available, the Ridge Cucumber can be grown. It is hardy, even in the north. No plant is more prolific, and so quickly do the fruits form that it will be necessary to look over the plants daily.

A sunny, open position, such as the balcony of a flat, is best for the plants where their handsome foliage will also prove attractive. All that is required is a box filled with decayed manure and loam. Sow the seed point upwards, covering the box with a sheet of clean glass.

Where growing in the open ground, if no cloche is available, make a miniature frame with bricks, and cover with a sheet of glass. Better still, remove the soil and fill to a depth of 8 in. with prepared manure. This is covered with 3 in. of soil which is made level with the surrounding ground. Similar miniature beds can be made at intervals of 4 ft., keeping them in line to help with cultivations. It is a better method than planting on ridges. It may be better to sow two seeds 1 in. deep, removing the weaker of the two plants when they have formed their second pair of leaves.

Should the garden be exposed to cold winds, the plants should be grown between ridges which will provide some protection. Planting should not be done on the top of the ridges, for in a dry summer the plants would lack moisture at the roots. If growing without any protection, sow the seed at the end of May in the north, early May in the south.

Stop the plants when they have formed two or three leaves, to encourage them to form lateral shoots which will carry the crop. To ensure a heavy crop, mulch either with decayed lawn mowings or decayed manure and never allow the plants to lack moisture. During a dry period and where growing in a light sandy soil, water copiously most days and this is best done in the evening.

VARIETIES

Bedfordshire Prize Ridge. It bears long fruits and is a heavy cropper; it is also hardy and crops well in most soils.

Burpee Hybrid. A fine hybrid from America bearing handsome, dark green fruits and cropping heavily in all seasons. The skin is smooth and thin, the flesh crisp and white.

Hampshire Giant. A hardy variety, the fruits growing more than 23 in. long, the skin pale green, the flesh white and of good flavour.

King of the Ridge. A well-grown plant will bear fruit up to 15 in., almost free of spines and of exceptional flavour. Possibly not quite as hardy as Stockwood Ridge, but otherwise one of the best.

Stockwood Ridge. The hardiest variety and most prolific, bearing long, well-shaped fruits and it does well in all soils.

Sutton's Prolific. Hardy and of compact habit, is suitable for small gardens, the medium-sized fruit possessing excellent flavour.

MORE HARDY CUCUMBERS

The Gherkin. A ridge cucumber, it bears short, spiny fruits which, if removed before they become too large, are excellent for pickling just as they are for they have a tender skin. They are also delicious eaten fresh if allowed to become slightly more mature. The fruit should be gathered every day at the height of the season.

The plants require the same conditions as for other ridge cucumbers, but where manure is scarce they will also crop abundantly if planted in ordinary friable soil, which has been manured for a previous crop. Give the plants a mulch as the season advances, whilst frequent applications of manure water will enhance the quality and cropping.

Apple Cucumber. In the opinion of connoisseurs of good food, this is the most delicious of all cucumbers.

The fruits are like pale yellow apples, oval in shape and should be gathered when they have reached apple size. Whilst the fruits possess the true cucumber flavour, they are much more juicy and yet the flesh is crisper.

In the north, grow the plants in a cold frame. In the south it is hardy and quick to mature and a frame is not necessary, but the plant is able to acquit itself to both frame and open ground culture.

The fruits are peeled and cut into slices, but to preserve the crisp juiciness, serve whole, to be cut the moment they are to be eaten with salad. Alternatively, peel and stew, and serve with white sauce with meats.

DANDELION

An unwanted weed in lawns, it is rarely cultivated, but its leaves are grown for use in winter and spring salads, being both nutritious and pleasantly bitter. It can be grown in shady situations. Sow seed in circles and as the leaves should be blanched before use (otherwise they tend to be too bitter), four or five plants should be allowed to remain in each clump to be covered with a rhubarb forcing pot, or with a deep box or large pot, for light must be excluded

The first plants will be ready for blanching twelve months from sowing the seed in March, ten days being required for the blanching. If several clumps are sown, they may be blanched at intervals as required, though no blanching should be done after the beginning of June, to enable the plants to recover and to build up their strength for the following year. After blanching, the leaves will be almost pure-white and about 12 in. long. They are cut off at soil level, and should be chopped and added to a bowl of spring lettuce. It is advisable to give the roots a compost mulch as soon as blanching has finished.

Sow the thick-leaved variety with its high vitamin A and iron content.

ENDIVE

See Chapter 5: 'Food from the Border'.

GARLIC

Garlic requires a light sandy soil, a position of full sun, and no manure. Two plantings are made, one in the south (but not in the north) towards the end of October, another in March, this also being the most suitable time for planting in the north. The bulbs should be separated and planted in clean ground, in drills made 12 in. wide and spacing them 6 in. apart in the rows. Plant 2 in. deep in a loose soil, this being one of the few plants that likes such a soil.

Bulbs planted in October will, in a favourable district, be ready for lifting late in July the following year, or before if required. Those planted in March are ready in the autumn. Lift as soon as the leaves turn yellow, the bulbs being dried on the ground if the soil is dry, or in an open shed. They are then strung together and hung up in a dry, frost-proof room for use when required.

Thompson & Morgan now market a specially selected Jumbo-size clove of up to 6 in. diameter which makes it easier to store and peel than the ordinary garlic. It is milder in flavour, and reaches maturity in a summer in which the ordinary garlic would find difficulty in ripening.

HAMBURG PARSLEY

This is a root, so named on account of its flavour being likened to that of parsley when cooked. In addition, its foliage also has a parsley flavour and remains green throughout winter so may be used for flavouring soups and fish, in place of parsley.

The roots are grown in exactly the same way as parsnips and nothing could be easier whilst the seedlings will also transplant readily and none should be wasted.

The plants like a long growing season, so sow the seed in March in a soil brought to a fine tilth and manured for a previous crop. Sow thinly in rows 15 in. apart, thinning out the young plants to 8 in. in the rows. A second sowing should be made in June for maturing early the following spring. During summer never allow the plants to lack moisture.

The roots are lifted at any time during winter and early spring; those from a later sowing being ready early the following summer.

KALE

There are numerous varieties of the kale; some are only ornamental, but others are of value as a winter vegetable. They were found in every cottage garden because of their hardiness, and the fact that they will crop well in almost all soils, provided it contains some humus. They will bear their shoots through winter, however severe. A soil which has been well manured for a previous crop, provided that it does not lack lime, and with the addition of one ounce per sq. yd. each of superphosphate and potash, is all that is necessary.

Seed is sown early in April, and the plants transplanted 20 in. apart towards the end of May. Plant firmly, and keep the hoe moving all summer. As they grow quite tall the soil should be trodden firmly around the stems during growth, for this will prevent them from being blown over by autumn winds.

The handsome curled leaves (its country name is Curly Kale) are removed whilst young and tender, stewing them rather than boiling to bring out their delicate flavour. The leaves will become stringy and coarse if allowed to grow too large.

VARIETIES

Cottager's Kale. Tall-growing, extremely hardy it produces an abundance of shoots for use in late winter and spring.

Labrador Kale. Probably the hardiest of all kales, producing its low mats of curled shoots through the severest winter and spring.

Moss Curled Kale. Very hardy and compact, with its fronds of moss-like foliage, delicious when steamed.

KOHL RABI

It is quick to mature, drought-resistant and hardy, yet few grow it. Three sowings should be made, the first early in April; the second mid-May; the third early July. Sown thinly in shallow drills 15 in. apart, the seedlings being thinned to 8 in. in the rows. The plants should be grown quickly, so that the roots are succulent when cooked, and used when the size of a large orange. Prepare the ground well and although this plant grows best in a sandy soil, it should be enriched with some decayed compost to retain moisture. Water whenever necessary, and although the plants will tolerate the driest of conditions, they are much more succulent when watered frequently.

Lift as required, but do not allow the plants to become too large.

The two best for garden culture are *Vienna White* and *Vienna Green*. The former is best for frame culture and is also the earliest to mature, the flesh being white and crisp. Vienna Green is the hardiest, and is sown for winter use.

LEEK

It has, since earliest times, been held in esteem everywhere, for it will survive the hardest winter and will grow in any soil as long as it is well drained. Do not manure heavily if the soil is in good heart from a previous crop. Like onions, leeks may be grown in the same ground year after year without deterioration.

Leeks should be trenched, removing the soil to a depth of 9 in. and to the width of a spade. Into the bottom is placed a layer of decayed garden refuse, and cover this with friable soil to which a quantity of peat has been added plus half an ounce each of superphosphate and sulphate of potash per yard of trench. Throw up the soil on either side as the trench is made, using the soil together with the fertilizer, from one side only, soil from the other side being used to blanch the leeks as they grow.

Seed is sown early in March in shallow drills. In cold gardens, a double row can be covered by cloches to start them off, for leeks need a long season to make large succulent 'sticks'. Sow in a friable soil containing some peat and coarse sand and if the seed is kept moist, it will soon germinate, the young plants being ready to plant out 1 July. Seed sown late, with the plants being set out at the end of July, will only result in small leeks. To transplant use a dibber and make a hole 1-2 in. deep, into which the plants are dropped. Do not fill in with soil, but water the trench after planting is done. A double row is made, the leeks being planted 6 in. apart, with the same distance between the rows. When planting, allow the wide part of the leaf to fall along, rather than across, the rows.

Never let the plants suffer from lack of water; like celery, leeks are great moisture lovers.

About the middle of August, corrugated paper is fastened (with an elastic band) around the lower part of the plants. This will help to 'draw' them, at the same time blanching the covered part. The paper will need renewing from time to time until the end of autumn.

The plants may be dug up as required, but as they are hardy enough to stand through winter, it is preferable to use them in March and April when vegetables are more scarce. Neither pest nor disease troubles the leek.

VARIETIES

Marble Pillar. Early to mature, it is a long-stemmed leek, and when blanched is tender and of mildest flavour.

Prizetaker. Though growing large, the pure white stems never lose their mild flavour.

The Lyon. An old favourite, it makes a large thick stem, free from any coarseness, and of rich flavour. It does well in all soils.

LETTUCE

Between rows of dwarf beans it may be grown as a 'catch' crop but requires a soil containing plenty of humus and one not lacking in lime. In wet weather, an acid soil will cause the plants to become slimy, and most town garden soils will have become acid through soot and sulphur deposits unless they have been well limed.

Lettuce does well under cloches or frames and its culture is given in the chapter dealing with these (see Chapter 8). For outdoors, sow seed thinly, either in a prepared seed bed for transplanting as soon as the seedlings can be handled, or where it is to mature. If there is overcrowding, some seedlings are removed and transplanted elsewhere. To provide a succession of lettuce in small numbers – which is better than making large plantings at any one time – sow a pinch of seed every month, selecting those varieties which are best for each season.

Lettuce does not fear cold; it is damp, foggy weather, often experienced November-December, which troubles it most, causing damping-off. For early supplies, seed is sown under cloches in February, for planting out in early April.

With outdoor lettuce, keep the plants growing from the moment the seed is sown, watering during periods of drought, but keeping the plants under glass dry in winter. In a soil lacking humus, the plants will quickly go to seed in hot, dry weather, whilst those under glass will damp off in winter if not kept dry and well-ventilated.

Too much nitrogen should not be given, otherwise the plants will not make good hearts, and during autumn and winter will tend to be soft, so falling a victim to mildew. This may be controlled by dusting plants under glass with flowers of sulphur every fortnight.

Always transplant in showery weather, when the ground is moist but not sticky. To plant when the soil is dry, even with watering afterwards, will cause wilting, from which plants may take many days to recover. Plants are best moved in the early stage, before they form a tap root. If this is not done, it is advisable to remove the tap root before re-planting for then the plants will heart better.

Plant on the flat, in rows 15 in. apart; allowing 18 in. for Webb's Wonderful.

VARIETIES

For summer, *Giant Crisphead* makes a large, tightly-folded heart of crisp texture and does not readily bolt in dry weather, whilst *Tennis Ball* makes a neat compact head of pale green and is sweet and juicy in a salad. *Salad Bowl*, with its fern-like leaves of yellowish green is of the endive type, the leaves being waved and curled. *Webb's Wonderful* is unrivalled as a family lettuce, with solid hearts as large as a football. Those who prefer a cos lettuce will find *Sugar Cos* both crisp and succulent, whilst *Jobjoit's Green* is best for autumn use.

MINT

This is a plant for the vegetable garden for unlike most herbs it prefers a moist, well-manured soil, so plant a few roots to provide sprigs to use with new potatoes and to make mint sauce. It will also grow well in semi-shade.

Spread out the creeping roots and plant them 2 in. deep, packing some peat about them before covering in with soil. This may be done in spring or autumn. Keep the soil moist and each year give the roots a mulch of sifted soil and decayed manure. In the first year remove only one or two sprigs from each root, cutting them off about 1 in. above ground.

In their second year, if a root is covered about 1 March with a barn cloche, there will be sprigs to cut for mint sauce to accompany early lamb.

SPECIES AND VARIETIES

There are three main forms of culinary mints: *Mentha viridis* or Spearmint, which is also Lamb Mint; *M. sylvestris,* the Hairy Mint; and *M. rotundifolia,* the Round-leaf Mint, the best form of which is *Bowle's Variety*. It is not affected by rust, which troubles so many of the mints. Another form of the Round-leaf Mint is the Apple Mint, readily distinguished from the other mints by its pale green shoots. These are also suitable for making mint sauces.

ONION

This is easy to grow from sets (bulbs) which is the best way to grow them north of the Trent where those grown from seed would not have time to reach maturity, unless raised in a propagator. Onions grown from sets are rarely attacked by the onion fly, and they will mature into large bulbs, even during a poor summer. If they have a fault it is their tendency to 'bolt', i.e. to run to seed, if allowed to suffer from lack of moisture.

To obtain large globular bulbs a long growing season is necessary, and a deeply-dug soil containing plenty of humus. As onions, like leeks, may be grown on the same ground year after year it is best to make a specially-prepared bed by deep digging and incorporating plenty of well-decayed manure or garden compost in winter. At the same time, work in two ounces per sq. yd. each of basic slag and sulphate of potash just before the sets are planted. Bring the bed to a fine tilth and allow it time to settle down before planting. Those who grow big onions for exhibition will roll the bed with a garden roller before planting, for onions must be grown in firm ground.

The sets are pressed into the soil, allowing 6 in. between the bulbs and 12 in. between the rows. The best variety to grow from sets is *Stuttgarter Riesen*, of which approximately three hundred sets weight one pound. It makes a large bulb which keeps well through winter, and will not readily 'bolt' in dry weather.

By late August the bulbs will be almost ripe, but to help them to ripen off during September, bend over the tops of the bulbs to prevent them forming seed. The bulbs are lifted towards the end of the month when the ground is dry, and laid out for twelve hours in the sun to complete the drying. Then clean them of any loose skin and remove the tops leaving only a small portion necessary to string them up and hang in a dry, airy shed, ready for use as required.

No summer salad is complete without its spring onions, seed of which is sown in drills early in October to stand through winter. By sowing in autumn it will be possible to lift the plants several weeks before those sown in spring.

Keep the ground free of all weeds where onions are grown, so make the drills wide enough for the hoe to be taken between the rows without damaging the plants.

If the rows are dusted with soot during the latter part of winter, this will bring additional warmth to the soil in spring. During a rainy day give a one ounce per yd. dressing of nitrate of soda between the rows, which will also encourage the plants to make some size.

Lift the plants as they swell, using the largest first. *White Lisbon* is the best variety; it is hardy enough to stand through winter and matures early, whilst it has a mild flavour.

The tree onion is a most useful plant and could be grown as a substitute for all other onions, to be pickled, or dried and used in stews, or chopped for use in salads. The plant produces clusters of five or six small bulblets, about the size of small shallots, at the tops of its branching stems. The bulbs may be used as required, or left to ripen to use through winter when they possess a delicate onion flavour.

The plants may be grown against a trellis by the side of a wall, or they may be planted in a bed where the stems are allowed to bend over, the bulblets taking root and forming a jungle of onions. They may be increased by removing the onions and planting exactly as for shallots. In this case it is advisable to plant the whole cluster together rather than to divide it up. September is the best time to plant, 12 in. apart. They will quickly root and in spring will grow away, producing their clusters of bulbs at the end of each stem.

PESTS AND DISEASES

Mildew. It is caused by a parasitic fungus and is most prevalent in a wet summer, appearing as pale brown spots on the leaves. Where the plants are badly attacked, the leaves heel over from the neck and die and the bulbs make no further growth. If observed, spray once every three weeks with weak Bordeaux mixture.

Onion Fly. The tiny flies lay their eggs on the necks of both onions and shallots, later small white grubs hatch out and tunnel into the bulbs making them useless for cooking. Their presence may be noticed by the leaves turning brown, but as prevention, dust the soil with calomel at planting time and take further precaution by dipping the bulbs into a paste made from calomel and water before planting out.

Onion sets are rarely troubled by this pest.

PARSNIP

The parsnip is appreciated by some but despised by others, for its flavour is pronounced, unlike that of any other root crop. It is hardy and happy in all soils, provided that the seed is sown in ground manured for a previous crop and brought to a fine tilth. As the seed is very short-lived, make sure that it is fresh each year.

The plants require a long season to mature, so seed is sown early in March in a deeply-worked soil, making the drills about 16 in. apart. It is important with parsnips to thin them out at an early stage to 4 in. apart and later to 8 in., for the roots grow large. They should be lifted through winter as required, or in cold parts lift in November and store in sand.

VARIETIES

Ryder's Exhibition. A handsome parsnip of mild flavour, the long, tapering root having a thin skin and milky-white flesh.

Ryder's Intermediate. The best variety for sowing where the soil is shallow, for the roots are thick and stumpy whilst the flavour is excellent.

The Student. It produces a root intermediate between the previous two varieties and is tender and richly flavoured.

PEA

The pea is best grown in a soil well prepared for a previous crop, but it also requires plenty of lime, and so the fertilizer that suits it better than any other is sewage sludge collected over lime (a source of manure which, however, is being gradually discontinued by the local authorities). Where this form of manure is now difficult to obtain, give the ground a liberal dressing of hydrated lime during early winter.

Peas require an open, sunny position and a soil containing moisture-holding humus rather than one rich in nitrogen, as excess nitrogen will lead the plants to form foliage and large deep green pods containing nothing but air and tiny peas. In any case peas make their own nitrogen. If peat is used to provide humus, additional lime should be given. Spent hops are also valuable, and at planting time give a one ounce per sq. yd. dressing of sulphate of potash, together with one ounce of superphosphate, to ensure early and satisfactory filling of the pods.

Peas make roots which extend deeply into the soil and are valuable in that they leave behind a soil enriched with nitrogen.

Make the first sowings early in November with round-seeded varieties, for the extra sweet Marrofat peas are wrinkled and hold the water in a wet winter. The wrinkles are there because a proportion of the starch content has been converted into sugar, this sweetness giving the pea a new popularity since the introduction of this type early last century. They make far superior eating to the round-seeded varieties. To sow, take out a trench 2 in. deep and the width of a spade. The soil at the bottom is dusted with potash and super-phosphate and the seeds are then planted separately, spacing them 2 in. apart. This allows the plants room to develop. In this way half a pint of seed (peas are usually sold in the pint measure) will sow a ten yard row.

As mice often prove troublesome with peas, winter varieties should be shaken up in a tin containing red lead and paraffin before planting. Take care to wash the hands after planting and destroy the rest of the red lead, or move it to a safe place away from children. To assist germination sprinkle peat over the seed before the trench is filled in. It is advisable to pass the covering soil through a sieve as it is replaced, so as to remove any stones.

When the row has been sown, put in the sticks on either side of the trench. This is a better method than waiting until the plants make growth, for then there is the chance of root disturbance and, if not staked within reasonable time, the plants will be almost impossible to stake well later, with resulting loss of crop.

Dwarf varieties require only small sticks, but there are certain peas of exceptional quality which attain a height of 6 ft. or more. For these, very stout stakes are required which should be pressed well into the ground. After staking, fish netting should be draped over the sticks to prevent birds attacking the succulent young peas as they appear. The plants will also grow up through the netting which will give extra support.

When planting more than one row of dwarf peas, allow at least 3 ft. between the rows. As a general rule, the distance allowed between the rows should equal the ultimate height of the plants – e.g., 5 ft. should be allowed between rows of 5 ft. tall varieties. For succession, sow the following:

Variety	Height	Sow	To mature
Early Bird	3 ft.	November	Late May
Early Onward	2 ft.	Early March	June
Advance Guard	2 ft.	Early April	Early July
Evergreen	3-4 ft.	Late April	Late July
Onward	2 ft.	Late April	Early August
Gladstone	3-4 ft.	Early May	Mid-August

PESTS AND DISEASES

Fusarium Wilt. The most troublesome disease of peas, attacking first the roots, then the stem, causing it to turn black. It is caused by badly drained soil and there is no cure, but on heavy land the resistant varieties should be grown.

Pea Mildew. It is most troublesome in dry weather and where present, the stems and leaves, later the pods, become covered in white powder and will greatly reduce the yield. If noticed, spray with weak Bordeaux mixture and repeat in three weeks.

Pea Moth. The moths lay in the flowers and on the leaves, the tiny white grubs entering the pods and devouring the peas making them unusable. To control, spray the plants with Sybol at fortnightly intervals from the time they come into bloom until the pods begin to swell.

VARIETIES

Early Bird. A round-seeded pea of great hardiness and suitable for autumn sowing in all soils. Height 3 ft.

Early Onward. It possesses the same freedom of cropping as Onward, and bears the same deep-green, blunt-nosed pods, tightly packed with peas. Height 2 ft.

Everbearing. It matures just before the maincrop peas and bears over a long period, the medium-sized pods appearing from each 'node' all the way up the stem. Height 3 ft.

Gladstone. A grand pea which has stood the test of time, the huge pods generally containing up to a dozen peas of excellent flavour. Height 3-4 ft.

Greensleeves. Of vigorous habit and bearing enormous crops of well-filled pods 6 in. long and of excellent flavour. It is highly resistant to disease. Height 3 - 4 ft. A less vigorous variety, known as Dwarf Greensleeves, is better suited to the small garden, and grows only 3 ft. high.

Kelvedon Wonder. One of the best all-round peas, it matures early, the well-filled pods of darkest green borne in profusion whilst it is highly resistant to fusarium wilt. Sow it in succession all summer. Height 2 ft.

Little Marvel. Of dwarf habit, it is a consistent cropper in the north, the dark green pods being borne in pairs and filling well. Height 2 ft.

Meteor. Round-seeded, it is quick to mature and a heavy cropper. Sow November. Height $1\frac{1}{2}$ ft.

Onward. A superb pea in every way, requiring little staking for the stems grow strong. The blunt-ended peas are borne in pairs and it crops heavily in all soils. Height 2 ft.

Petit Pois. For flavour, this must be one of the best peas. Growing to a height of 3-4 ft. it bears heavy crops. Sow in April, planting the seed 4 in. apart in the trenches.

Gather the pods as soon as they are filled, and steam as they are. The peas will readily leave the pods after cooking and will have retained their entire flavour.

Recette. Its introduction heralded a break-through in that from each node, three pods are produced instead of Onward's two and the one of older varieties, each pod filled with eight or nine richly flavoured peas.

Sleaford Three Kings. A triple-podded wrinkle-seeded pea maturing a week after Onward. The pods grow to 4 in. long and contain eight or nine dark green peas of excellent flavour. Height 2-3 ft.

Sugar Pea. A pea with a difference and more like a bean, for both pod and seed are eaten together. They are stringless and are tender if gathered young and eaten fresh. They crop better in the south than in the north, except in a warm, sunny summer when they seem to do well anywhere. The seeds require the same culture as for ordinary peas and attain a height of only 15 in., bearing an abundance of pods through August.

Sutton's Evergreen. It has recently received an Award of Merit for it is of strong constitution, its dark green pods being borne in pairs and tightly filled. Height 3-4 ft.

POTATO

The ability of the potato to crop well, provided that it is manured, in weed infested land is an additional value of this important food crop. Owing to the process of lifting and general cultivation, the soil goes through a rigorous cleaning, when all perennial weeds are eliminated and the soil reduced to a fine tilth. As the ground should also have been manured for the potatoes, it will be in condition to grow peas or beans the following year.

Sprouted tubers will increase the yield and, with early potatoes, will ensure they mature as early as possible, depending upon soil and situation. Sprouting should be commenced early in the new year and for this a frost-proof room is essential. It is also necessary to obtain the tubers from a reliable source. A stone of potato seed, certified as grown in Ireland or Scotland (that grown on high ground in the north of England is almost as good) will yield from one hundred to two hundred pounds of potatoes depending on how well the crop is grown.

Sprouting is done by placing the tubers on end in a shallow wooden box lined with 1 in. of damp peat. At one time, growers would cut the tubers and dip them in lime but potatoes do not like lime, which encourages scab. Place the boxes in a light place but away from strong sunlight and protected from frost.

In a late spring, when the ground is cold and wet and planting has to be delayed until soil conditions are suitable, the tubers continue to grown unharmed and will soon catch up when planted.

If the tubers have more than two 'sprouts', retain only the two strongest and rub off any others.

With sprouted potatoes, a crop may be expected at least three weeks earlier than with unsprouted seed, and a twenty pounds heavier crop may be expected owing to the longer growing period from every stone of seed.

Early potatoes should be planted as soon as climate and soil conditions permit. This may be as early as February in sheltered gardens in the south-west, or as late as mid-April in the colder northern climate. Late March or April will prove suitable for the second earlies and maincrop in favourable areas.

To plant, first make a trench to a depth of 8 ins., and to the width of a spade. Make the trenches 2 ft. apart, for the maincrop, to allow for earthing up. At the bottom, spread some well-decayed farmyard manure to a depth of 3 in. This is covered with 1 in. of peat and on this the tubers are planted 2 ft. apart. The trenches for the early crop need be no more than 18 ins. apart, and the tubers set the same distance apart in the rows. Do not plant too close as this will cause the top growth (the haulm) to become drawn and the potatoes will be small as a result, whilst fungus disease will be prevalent. Do not plant too soon. Wait until the soil is friable and beginning to warm up. Remember the old adage, 'plant late potatoes early and early potatoes late'!

When planting the tubers, take care not to break off the sprouts. Cover them with more peat or some friable soil, and to the soil which will be used to fill up the trench add two ounces per yd. of a mixture of superphosphate and sulphate of potash. This will not only increase the yield, but will build up a plant showing considerable resistance to disease. The mixture should be in the proportion of two-thirds superphosphate to one-third potash. Artificial nitrogenous manures are not to be recommended, for in a wet season they encourage excessive top growth more liable to disease whilst the tubers tend to become dark when cooked.

If the land is low-lying or of a heavy nature, the tubers are best planted on ridges. The soil is taken out in V-fashion and a drill 6 in. deep is made at the top of the ridge, in which the tubers are planted.

When planting, select a position where the plants can enjoy

full sun, for they are never happy in shade.

As the foliage appears above the soil, earthing up should be done at regular intervals, and as a precaution against blight spray the foliage with Bordeaux mixture about 1 July, and again at the end of the month.

A reliable indication that the crop is ready for lifting is when the foliage begins to die down, although earlies may be lifted as soon as the tubers have grown to a reasonable size. Lift with a fork, taking care to place it well away from the centre of the plant so as not to damage the tubers. They are then placed in a deep bucket or barrow lined with a sack, which is used to cover the potatoes to exclude light. Lift when the soil is dry and friable, for the potatoes will not keep if wet. Potatoes lifted for early use will not, of course, be stored, although it is advisable to keep them in the dark, under the stairs or in a cellar. Maincrop varieties for home consumption will keep well if placed on a layer of straw in any frost-proof building, but they must be kept away from light if they are not to turn green.

'New' potatoes may be enjoyed all the year round, and are never more appreciated than at Christmas time – for which purpose a number may be placed in a metal biscuit tin containing dry peat, and buried 12 in. deep in the garden, with a large stone marking their position. The time to do this is when they are right for lifting in summer.

PESTS AND DISEASES

Blight. A common disease of potatoes, brown marks appearing on the leaves, often when the summer is damp and humid. Later, the stems turn black and the plant has an unpleasant smell. As a precaution, spray with Bordeaux mixture when the foliage is about 8 in. high and again a month later.

Colorado Beetle. A 'notifiable' pest, it measures about half an inch and has orange and black striped wings. Wintering below the soil, it emerges in spring to lay its orange eggs on the foliage when the grubs can soon wipe out a plantation. Before planting, treat the soil with Aldrin dust which will also prevent an attack by the Flea Beetle which has yellow and black stripes down its back.

Leaf Roll. A virus disease caused by aphis when the leaves turn brown and curl up. The whole plant takes on a stunted appearance and few tubers are formed. There is no cure but, to be on the safe side, plant certified tubers of Irish or Scottish origin.

Wart. Also known as Black Scab, it is a 'notifiable' disease for which there is no cure. Upon lifting, the tubers show cauliflower-like growths, often black and will have become mummified. They must be burned at once and fresh ground used for future plantings. Where there has been an outbreak, plant only wart-immune varieties.

VARIETIES – FIRST EARLIES

Di Vernon. It makes a handsome waxy-fleshed tuber, creamy-white, shaded with mauve, and is a heavy bearer. It has an attractive 'earthy' flavour.

Pentland Beauty. A 'red' potato which is oval and pink-skinned, with shallow eyes and makes only short haulm. It is the heaviest cropper of all the earlies.

Sharpe's Express. The best early for heavy soils, in which it crops heavily, the kidney-shaped tubers having pale golden flesh and being richly flavoured.

SECOND EARLIES

Valuable to bridge the gap between the early and maincrop varieties.

Craig's Royal. In the dry summer of 1975 it cropped better than any variety. The white kidney tubers with pinkish-red shading about the eyes are of handsome appearance whilst it cooks 'floury' and is of splendid flavour.

Dunbar Rover. A reliable cropper in light soil. The tubers are white and oval, the flesh pure white, this being a delicious variety for baking. It is immune to wart disease.

MAINCROP

Arran Comrade. A round potato, the white tubers are covered with a faint netting. Raised by Donald MacKelvie on his Isle of Arran croft, it is the finest of the 'Arrans', in that it crops heavily and makes delicious eating cooked in its jacket.

Desirée. A red-skinned potato of recent introduction which crops heavily and keeps until June when the first earlies will be ready. It cooks to a deep golden colour like Golden Wonder when baked in its skin.

Golden Wonder. A hundred years old and unsurpassed for quality and flavour – which might be described as being somewhere between that of a chestnut and an artichoke. It is, however, a light cropper unless grown well and in a soil which suits it.

Kerr's Pink. A hardy variety, late to mature and though an old one still a firm favourite. It does well in a heavy soil and in moist western districts. The tubers are round and pale pink. It keeps well and is of excellent flavour.

King Edward VII. Raised in Northumberland at the beginning of the century, this pink-skinned, kidney-shaped variety possesses its own delicious flavour which has maintained its popularity. A red-skinned form called Red King is equally delicious. Both keep well through winter and spring but are not immune to wart disease.

Majestic. This almost fool-proof variety crops heavily in all soils, whilst its rounded tubers are immune to wart disease. It cooks 'floury' and is splendid to eat, being one of the best potatoes ever introduced.

Maris Piper. Of recent introduction, it does not make a very big tuber, being round and creamy white but it cooks to a deep golden colour and has outstanding flavour.

Pentland Crown. It bears a heavy crop of white kidney-shaped potatoes in all soils and keeps well.

RADISH

They are best sown broadcast in a raised bed which has been prepared in winter, incorporating some humus so that, if the summer is warm and dry, the plants will not lack moisture. Old mushroom bed compost is ideal for radishes, but a mixture of peat and used hops or well-decayed farmyard manure is also valuable. Dig the ground deeply, then allow the soil to become pulverized by frost. In March the bed can be raked to a fine tilth and stones removed.

Sow the seed thinly and when the soil is friable, rake it into the surface. Never allow the plants to lack moisture, for if so the radishes will be hard and bitter through taking too long to mature. Radishes must be grown quickly to be sweet and tender.

VARIETIES

For outdoors, *Cherry Belle* is quick to mature, forming a round root of cherry-red with crisp white flesh. Also good is *French Breakfast*, its red cylindrical root being tipped with white; and *Sparkler*, its round root being half red, half white whilst Thompson & Morgan's *Red Prince* makes a large round root with ice white flesh.

RADISH, WINTER

Few know the Black Winter radish, let alone grow it, but it was grown in Tudor times and Stuart gardeners included it in winter salads.

Sow the seed at the end of July, in drills 12 in. apart and in a soil well manured for a previous crop. It makes a round root almost like a small turnip, and is black-skinned, but the flesh is pure white and succulent if grown well, and is in no way stringy. Sliced or grated into a salad, it has a nutty flavour and is without any of the bitterness so often found in summer radishes.

Thin the seedlings to 6 in. apart in the rows and keep well watered through summer. Late in October, lift the roots and store in dry sand to be used through winter. There is a long form, also quite black which requires the same culture, but if the soil is heavy or stoney it is not as satisfactory as the round form.

Those who are put off from growing a winter radish by the appearance of the black variety should try *China Rose*. It requires the same culture, the seed being sown in July in drills, and is lifted and stored in the same way. It is like a large *French Breakfast*, of blunt tubular form, thickening near the base. The colour is vivid cerise-red with the flesh white, cool and crisp.

SEAKALE BEET

Silver Beet it is also called, and though rarely seen today in the cottage garden, it was at one time a real favourite. Unlike the Spinach Beet, it will crop well in a poorly-manured soil if the soil is of a heavy nature and is able to retain summer moisture. It may be helped by working in a small quantity of peat.

It is of vigorous habit and should be thinned to 12 in. in the rows which are made 18 in. apart. The seed is sown in late May, so that the plants will make plenty of leaf by autumn, when it is most wanted.

As with all beet — except the non-bleeding beetroot — the Seakale Beet should have its leaves removed by twisting rather than by cutting. The thick fleshy stems are stewed or steamed; the leaf part being cooked like spinach. The variety *Vintage Green* is outstanding, the leaves remaining green until Christmas.

SHALLOT

One of the easiest of vegetables to grow, it is used for pickling, to provide a welcome addition to rissoles and winter meats. The bulbs require a soil containing some decayed manure, the ground being prepared during winter when the surface will be broken up to a fine tilth by the frosts. In March rake in two ounces per sq. yd. of sulphate of potash, and roll or tread to ensure a firm bed.

Shallots are one of the earliest crops to be planted, as soon as the soil is right, some time in March, the small bulbs being pressed into the surface but in no way covered. Plant 9 in. apart each way, and keep the bed free from weeds and the surface stirred up so that air and moisture can reach the roots. The bulbs must be kept well supplied with water through summer.

Towards the end of August, bend over the necks to encourage ripening, and at the end of September, the clusters of small bulbs are lifted and dried. To bring out the maximum amount of flavour they should be stored in a dry room for a month, but no longer, before being pickled.

The best variety is called *Giant Red-Skinned*. Where possible use Dutch bulbs, which will have been specially grown for seed purposes, and will have enjoyed a long ripening season.

SPINACH

Its unique flavour is not to everyone's taste but it has health-giving qualities and there may be some who would like to grow it.

For summer use it is best grown from a succession of sowings, beginning with the first about mid-March. To prevent the plants running to seed, select a position of dappled shade (such as between rows of other vegetables) and provide a humus-laden soil. The plants should be grown as coolly as possible and if allowed to become dry at the roots they will quickly run to seed.

As it is required to obtain an abundance of leaf, and in the quickest possible time, work into the soil some nitrogenous manure, and give the plants half an ounce per sq. yd. dressing of nitrate of soda when they have made some growth.

Seed is sown in shallow drills 12 in. apart, the plants being thinned to 9 in. in the rows. It is the round-leaf varieties which are grown for summer use, sowings being made every three weeks until the end of July, whereafter and until late September, sowings are made of the winter or 'prickly' spinach.

So that winter spinach does not decay, grow in a raised bed of sufficient width to take five rows, each 12 in. apart, so that picking may be done from either side of the bed without treading the soil.

Gather the leaves when young, before they become too coarse, and as soon as the plants run to seed, remove them.

SUMMER VARIETIES

Monstrous Viroflay. Strangely named, but a valuable round-leaf variety making a large plant and excellent for the deep freeze.

Monnopa. This is the spinach with low oxalic acid content and now grown for baby food. Its flavour is mild whilst it is 'bolt' resistant and hardy enough to stand through winter.

Nobel. The heaviest cropper of the summer varieties, the leaves being large and fleshy with pronounced flavour after cooking.

WINTER VARIETIES

Hollandia. The long, deep-green leaves are arrow-shaped, and most attractive in the border. A most prolific variety, the flavour mild.

Standwell. Named for its hardiness and for an abundance of large, succulent leaves which it continues to produce through winter.

SPINACH, NEW ZEALAND
See Chapter 5: 'Food from the Border'.

SWEET CORN
Indian Corn or Corn-on-the-Cob, as it is also called, requires a long season to mature, the seed best being sown under glass or

over a hotbed about 1 March. The plants also need the minimum of root disturbance and are best raised in Root-o-pots from the beginning. The young plants should not be hardened off too soon; mid-May is early enough to begin the process if they are to be planted out unprotected, so that they will be ready to go out about 1 June – a week later in the north. Where barn cloches are used, the plants may go out early in May from an early March sowing, having been partly hardened off early in May. The value of barn cloches is in providing shelter from cold winds, which the sweet corn will not tolerate, for the cloches may be placed on their sides and kept in position long after the plants have reached the top glass, which is removed early in June. The use of barn cloches will ensure success with this crop, the cobs ripening by early August, by the month end in the north, a full month earlier than those planted out without protection.

Sweet corn needs a rich soil and a sunny position, but one where the plants will be protected from winds. If no glass is used, it is advisable to erect a row of wattle hurdles or corrugated iron sheeting on the northern side, or against the prevailing wind. The plants detest winds.

Having selected a position, soil preparation should begin early in spring, digging in as much humus as possible. Sweet corn thrives on shoddy, whilst spent hops are also of value. Decayed strawy manure, or that from old mushroom beds is suitable, and give a handful of bone meal to each square yard. Indian Corn is a form of grass, and like all grasses it must have nitrogen to grow well. Peat may also be used to give humus to the soil, in addition to the manure, whilst the soil must not lack lime.

Where cloches are used, place the glass over the ground ten days before planting, to warm the soil so that there will be no check to plant growth. The cloches may later be turned on their sides around the plants to give protection from cold winds when the plants have reached the top. When the soil is in a friable condition the plants are set out 18 in. apart in the open, 12 in. apart under cloches, a double row being planted under a 2 ft. wide barn cloche. Water in well after planting, and from early July give copious waterings with liquid manure twice each week until the cobs have finished swelling. This will make them grow large and succulent. Keep the hoe moving between the rows and give a mulch of strawy manure at the beginning of July, for the roots must never lack moisture.

The plants produce the male flower at the top but the flowers which are to form the cob, the females, develop from the leaf joints at the bottom of the plant, the silky tassels catching the grains of pollen as they fall from above. Though the plants should not be unduly cramped when set out, the closer they are planted, the better will the cob-forming flowers be pollinated.

Choosing the right time for gathering the cobs will call for some care. On no account must the seeds be allowed to become too hard in the cob. The seeds must have matured, be firm and yet still be juicy, the cobs being almost like a short ridge-cucumber in size. Where they have been grown in the open unprotected, the cobs will be ready for removing early September, but if the summer has lacked warmth, they may have to depend on a good autumn to mature and it may be about 1 October before they are ready.

By then the plants will have made considerable height, perhaps to 6 ft., so it will be advisable to fix stakes at the ends of the rows during August, and to pass strong twine down each row. This will prevent the weight of foliage and fruit from breaking the stems.

VARIETIES

The F1 Hybrid varieties have been raised especially for the British climate and are hardier and earlier to mature than older strains.

Early King. The earliest to mature, it forms a broad cob 8 in. long, well filled and of excellent flavour.

Kelvedon Glory. The best variety for southern gardens, it follows Early King, bearing pale yellow cobs 8 in. long, and is of delicious flavour. It perhaps ripens too late for the north.

North Star. The best for northern gardens, it received an Award of Merit at the Royal Horticultural Society Trials (1969). It will mature even in a cold summer, and bears large broad cobs 8 in. long, packed with golden corn.

Polar V. An excellent new variety for northern gardens as it matures quickly, but since it produces its pollen early, plant 2 in. closer together than other varieties.

TOMATO
See Chapter 8: 'Food from a Frame'.

TURNIP
Its culture under glass for an early crop is given in 'Food from a Frame' (Chapter 8). For outdoors make a sowing early in April to mature in early July, lifting the roots before they become too large. They must be given a rich, deeply-dug soil and a firm seed bed. Thin to 6 in. as soon as large enough to handle and never allow the plants to suffer from lack of moisture, otherwise they will grow coarse and woody.

For winter, sow in July, as described for a spring sowing. It is not advisable to sow before this time, otherwise the roots will become too large and coarse. Completely hardy, they are lifted as required.

VARIETIES
For winter, sow *Golden Ball,* with its sweet yellow flesh, which may be allowed to stand until the new year, and for summer, *Early Snowball* matures as quickly in the open as it does under glass.

VEGETABLE MARROW
See Chapter 8: 'Food from a Frame'.

CHAPTER SEVEN

GROWING FOOD IN A SMALL GREENHOUSE

It is not necessary to have a garden to possess a greenhouse. One can enjoy out of season and early crops by erecting in a courtyard or even on a terrace adjoining the house a small lean-to greenhouse which in winter may be used as a sunroom. Much enjoyment can be obtained from a greenhouse correctly sited in which tomatoes, cucumbers and mouth-watering melons can be grown. On the back wall of a lean-to, a peach or nectarine can be trained so that it will eventually cover it; and a vine over the roof. During winter, chrysanthemums in pots can be taken inside to bloom until the new year, followed by early bulbs to provide colour until it is time for the tomato crop, thus using the greenhouse all the year.

TYPES OF GREENHOUSE

Where the conventional type greenhouse in cedarwood to stand on a brick base is required, those manufactured by Walton's of Newark-on-Trent and by Pratten's of Bath are to be recommended. I have used them for years and they have proved most efficient and trouble-free. Pratten's also make the Trimline Dutch-type house of aluminium construction. It is 8 ft. 2 in. long and 6 ft. 2in. wide and has a sliding door at one end. Benches can be erected on either side or tomatoes, cucumbers and other crops can be planted directly into ground beds. It is supplied with roof ventilators and is suitable for raising vegetable seedlings and bedding plants in spring. Messrs. Alton's of Bewdley also manufacture excellent aluminium and cedarwood greenhouses of similar style, and a lean-to in the same materials.

A lean-to, however, should be erected only against a sunny wall for apart from the forcing of rhubarb in winter, most greenhouse crops must have plenty of light and warmth provided by the sun and this also means greater economy in heating. Crittall-Hope make a splendid lean-to, the large model being 9 ft. 6 in. high at the back which gives ample room for a peach or vine, whilst it is 9 ft. in width with a sliding door. Staging supports are obtainable and also shelf brackets. Early bulbs can be brought on beneath the staging and at the back, tomatoes (followed by chrysanthemums) planted directly into ground beds of prepared soil. Made for easy assembly, the metal is protected by the hot-dip galvanizing process and glass, putty and glazing clips are provided. A sliding door with finger tip control gives easy access.

A most satisfactory and inexpensive greenhouse may be obtained from Garden Relax Limited of Rainham, Essex. A strong galvanized metal frame is fixed to the ground and over the frame is placed Hi-clarity ICI plastic sheeting. This is shatter-proof and should be used where there are low flying aircraft, whilst the growing conditions are the equal of a glass house. There is built-in ventilation and staging is supplied. Erection takes only a few minutes and, if required, the greenhouse can quickly be taken down for use elsewhere.

It is possible to erect a simple lean-to by using 2 in. timber for the uprights and roof and covering them with PVC sheeting of heavy quality or with Screenet, a polythene sheeting reinforced with wire netting. A simple door frame may be constructed of laths and this is fastened to an upright at one end by two strong hinges. Including the cost of the covering, the lean-to may be constructed for less than £20, even using new timber and including staging.

Where space is so restricted that the conventional type of greenhouse is difficult to erect, the circular house manufactured by Humex Limited is recommended. It is 7 ft. high, is 8 ft. in diameter and is topped by a dome 3 ft. in diameter which can be raised to provide top ventilation in addition to the all-round intake of fresh air at ground level. Instant shading is by roller blinds in green PVC material and takes only seconds to manipulate. Staging provides support for plants at all levels. If required, it is heated by a close coiled mineral-insulated copper-sheathed cable, providing an all-round even distribution of heat which will increase the temperature at least 25°F. above outside temperatures.

METHODS OF HEATING

Thought should be given to heating the greenhouse. This may be by electricity where the greenhouse is situated close to the home, though electricity is now expensive and is always liable to be cut off at a time when outside temperatures are at their lowest. To-day, paraffin oil heating is efficient and still inexpensive whilst there is no danger of it being cut off unless through one's own carelessness.

A highly efficient electric heater is the Autoheat, manufactured by Findlay, Irvine Limited of Penicuik, Scotland. With the 3000 watt model, large enough to heat a greenhouse 12 ft. by 8 ft., there is a built-in thermometer and thermostatic control ensures the most efficient running possible. The cylindrical heater is made of rigid PVC which will not rust, whilst all metal parts are earthed. A continuous air flow maintains a buoyant atmosphere and keeps condensation to a minimum, It also helps prevent mildew and botrytis which are encouraged by a stagnant atmosphere. The heater can be set at the required temperature which is controlled by the thermostat.

Ekco, the television set manufacturers, market efficient horticultural thermotubes for fixing beneath a greenhouse bench or in a garden room and also a thermostat for temperature control. They are rust- and drip-proof and have die-cast terminal chambers. They carry a load of 60 watts per foot and are obtainable in lengths of up to 12 ft. which, at this size, cost little more than 50p a foot.

Another efficient heater is the Parwin P70, made of rust-proof steel. Its three elements are doubly insulated to prevent shorting through the case, thus eliminating dangers from condensation, whilst the thermostat, two-way switch and mains cable entry are enclosed in a drip-proof chamber. The 3 kw model will give frost-proof protection for a greenhouse 20 ft. by 12 ft., whilst the two-way switch allows for the stopping and starting of the cir-

culation fan as the thermostat switches the heating elements off
and on.

Paraffin heating provides a suitable alternative and the Aladdin
blue-flame greenhouse heater is most efficient. The 2 in. burner
model heats a greenhouse of 100 cu. ft. for about 3p an hour.
Their Maxi-heater unit will provide heat for a week without
re-filling, for the paraffin is stored in a five-gallon tank from
which there is a feed to the heater. If the wick is kept trimmed,
there will be no trouble with smoking whilst heat distributors,
fitted to the sides, help to circulate warmth evenly.

The Eltex 'Malvern' heaters are also to be recommended. The
smaller model is designed to heat a greenhouse 10 ft. by 6 ft; the
larger model will heat one 15 ft. by 10 ft. and will burn for
approximately a day and a half without re-filling. They are
strongly constructed of galvanized steel sheeting with a brass
burner.

The use of soil warming cables in a heated greenhouse for raising tomato and other plants and propagating cuttings will enable
the air temperature to be much reduced and so prove more
economical. The bottom heat generated by the cables will keep
the young plants growing when outside temperatures are low,
but soil warming cables should be used in conjunction with other
greenhouse heating. A low voltage transformer unit which
reduces the mains supply to a low safe voltage is used to heat a
plastic covered galvanized wire under a bed of soil or sand.

Another inexpensive method of raising seedlings is by means of
horticultural heater tape as manufactured by Agriflex. A 30 ft.
length of cable will carry a load of 80 watts and is readily clipped
to the underside of a greenhouse bench. The flexible glass-
covered element is encased in heat-resisting PVC to form a
waterproof heating element and 30 ft. of tape costs less than £5,
with running costs extremely low.

A propagating unit, again with low running costs, may be used
inside the greenhouse to increase the temperature in a concentrated area. In a temperature of 65°F. (18°C.) which is readily
maintained by the unit, tomato seed will germinate in about
seven days from a January sowing; cucumber seed in five days in
a temperature of 70°F. (21°C.) To maintain these air
temperatures in a greenhouse would be expensive and inefficient,

for the cost of a propagating unit is small and it will have a long life, to be used over and over again for raising seedlings which need high temperatures for their satisfactory germination.

An efficient propagating unit is the Autogrow P40 with thermostatic control. Made with a galvanized base and a polythene cover, it measures 30 in. by 16 in. and is 3 in. deep with a 12 in. high cover. It holds seed trays which are specially made for it. A heating element rated at 15 watts per sq. ft. and an 18 in. rod thermostat built into the base provide reliable and economic heat.

After sowing, connect to the mains, turn the knob to the required temperature and wait for the seeds to germinate, keeping the compost moist. One light indicates that the supply is 'on' whilst the other comes 'on' and 'off' with the heating element to enable one to see if it is working correctly. Rapid germination will ensure that damping-off is reduced to a minimum. After germinating and when the seedlings are ready to leave the propagator, they are grown-on in lower temperatures so that they become sturdy.

The Humex automatic propagator may also be recommended. Measuring 36 in. by 20 in. and 12 in. deep, it is constructed of fibreglass and is entirely automatic, the temperature being regulated by a rod-type thermostat which can be adjusted to give any temperature up to 180°F. (82°C.) For safety, the low-voltage heating wire is enclosed in a layer of sand. On a 40-watt consumption, its running costs are less than 10p a week which is a big saving when compared to raising plants in a greenhouse heated to the necessary temperature for seed germination.

Adco have put on the market a low consumption (14 watts) propagating unit which provides bottom heat for seed trays, especially those made of plastic. Efficient and inexpensive to run, it is not as large as the other units described but is adequate for raising small numbers of seedlings.

SUITABLE COMPOSTS

Before the seedlings are ready to transplant, have on hand the pots or containers into which they are to be moved. Vacapots, thin-walled plastic containers divided into twenty-four compartments 1 in. square and filled with compost, are recommended for growing-on the seedlings which should be moved from the propagating unit when large enough to handle. They will remain in the Vacapot trays until ready to move to Jiffypots which are compressed pots made of a suitable growing medium. The pots are filled with compost in the usual way and when full of roots, they will then grow into the high grade sphagnum peat moss and wood pulp from which the pots are made. Root-o-pots, made in Eire of finest quality Irish peat and woodfibre are equally efficient. 'Junior' size pots are about $2\frac{1}{4}$ in. round and cost about £1 a hundred. If the plants are to be moved to larger pots for growing-on, all that is necessary is to plant each exactly as it is. There will be no root disturbance and so no check to growth.

For seed sowing, use the John Innes sowing compost. This is obtainable from most nurserymen and garden shops but make sure that it is fresh, otherwise it may be contaminated by weed seeds or fungus spores, whilst the superphosphate, so necessary to promote healthy and vigorous root action, soon loses strength.

The John Innes sowing compost is made up of: two parts sterilized loam, one part peat, one part sand, one and a half ounces superphosphate of lime, three-quarters of an ounce ground limestone, per bushel.

Introduce the compost to the warmth of the greenhouse a few days before it is to be used. Line the boxes or pans with damp moss then add the compost to a depth of 2 in., allowing just sufficient room at the top for watering. Sow the seed thinly, cover with a sprinkling of compost and water gently. Then place the box in the propagator and turn on the current. Never allow the compost to dry out or germination will be delayed. As soon as the surface appears to be drying, give a gentle watering with a fine rose or syringe.

For growing-on the plants after transplanting, use the John Innes potting compost which is of increased strength. This is made up of: seven parts sterilized loam, three parts peat, two parts sand, three-quarters of an ounce limestone, half a pound J. I. base, per bushel.

The base is made up of: two parts hoof or horn meal, two parts superphosphate of lime, one part sulphate of potash.

This provides a balanced diet for the growing plants. If making up one's own compost, do not exceed the stated amounts for it has been established that plants in the seedling stage grow better in a slightly acid compost than in one that is alkaline in reaction.

Soil-less composts, several of which are on the market, are made up of peat and sand with added nutrients and though light to handle, they require far more attention with their watering, and after using them for several years, I have returned to the John Innes composts with much better results.

TRANSPLANTING SEEDLINGS

It is important that when seedlings are raised indoors, there should be no delay when they are ready for transplanting, and it is also important to have the greenhouse heated to not less than 55°F. (13°C) so that the plants can grow-on without check. Tomatoes and cucumbers which are to be grown-on in the greenhouse will need no hardening-off but those to be planted outside should first be hardened in a cold frame or in deep boxes covered with glass at night.

The plants should not go out for hardening until 1 May and should have two to three weeks' hardening before being planted out. French and runner beans (also cauliflower and leek plants which need a long season to develop to any size and are best raised under glass) will also require hardening, though they are hardy enough to stand through a severe winter.

A word about transplanting seedlings. They should be moved as soon as they have formed their second pair of leaves. If left too long in the sowing compost, they will become 'drawn', grow spindly and never recover. To transplant, hold the plant with the fingers of one hand and use the other hand to gently prise up the roots with a small piece of wood or cane made smooth at one end. Have the newly filled containers ready and at hand so that the plant can be re-planted with the minimum of movement and delay. Make a hole in the compost in which to drop the seedling. Then its roots should be nicely covered by the compost and made firm by gently pressing the compost with the fingers. When transplanting is complete, water in the seedlings and place them as near the glass as possible.

Timing is all-important in sowing indoors. To sow too soon in the year, during January perhaps, will prove expensive, for the weather will usually be too cold to rely on the natural warmth of the sun to provide any worthwhile heat. On the other hand, sowing too late will mean that greenhouse plants expected to crop at least a month before plants grown in the open begin to crop, will be too late and the value of the greenhouse will be lost. Late sowing, too, will mean that tomatoes or cucumbers will occupy the house at a time when other plants should be coming on. Late chrysanthemums, for example, will bloom until the year end and in their turn will be cleared before sowing time for tomatoes and for the bringing-on of dahlia cuttings. In this way the greenhouse will be kept in constant use and the production of food crops can go hand-in-hand with that of flowers to brighten the garden and home.

When watering greenhouse plants, it is preferable to use rainwater which has been allowed to stand several hours in the can before it is used. This will take off the chill; if the water is used cold, it will cause a check to the seedlings growing in a warm greenhouse. Rainwater may be collected in a barrel outside the greenhouse, at the opposite end to the doorway. A length of plastic guttering to catch the water as it falls on the roof and a short length of down pipe will take the water to the barrel from which the can or cans may always be kept filled.

Greenhouse cleanliness is most important. In autumn, make sure that the glass or PVC sheeting is neither cracked nor broken, which would cause heat-loss during winter and be most uneconomic. Also, wash down the glass or sheeting with soapy water to remove any grime which would keep out valuable sunlight in winter. At this time it is a wise precaution to spray the inside with a Ster-Izal solution to kill any pests and fungus diseases.

If electricity is used for heating, install a light bulb so that it will be possible to see to the plants in the evening during winter, for it will be dark when you return home from work and a greenhouse can give much pleasure at this time of year when the weather is usually too cold for outside gardening. If a disc impregnated with a pesticide (or fungicide) is placed over the bulb, the heat of the bulb will release the fumigant and keep the plants clean and healthy. It is a simple precaution costing very little. Ensure that all pots and boxes used for sowing seeds are scrubbed frequently; also the bench if made of wood for it is here that pests and disease may hide. Out-of-season food crops are now so valuable that all factors adverse to their successful culture must be eliminated.

Food Plants to Grow Under Glass

AUBERGINE

Because of the shape of its fruit, it is also known as the egg-plant and although native to Mexico and the southern United States, it may readily be grown in the British Isles, in a cold or heated greenhouse.

The seed is sown in January in John Innes sowing compost. In a temperature of 56°F. (13°C.) it will quickly germinate. Just cover the seed after sowing and place in a propagator.

When large enough to handle, transplant the seedlings to small pots containing John Innes potting compost and again to larger pots three to four weeks later. When the plants are established, nip out the growing point to encourage bushy growth. By this time, artificial heat will be necessary only at night. In early May, the plants will require copious amounts of water and ample ventilation, and as they love the sunlight, should be placed as near to the glass as possible. On sunny days, syringe the foliage as often as possible though always ensuring that it will have dried off by nightfall. Syringing will help the fruit to set and when the first fruits have formed, feeding once weekly with dilute manure water will increase the yield and size and improve the quality of the fruit.

When giving the plants their final potting, use a well-drained loam containing some sand to keep it porous and mix in about one-third by bulk of decayed manure. Old mushroom bed compost, obtainable from growers who advertise it in the gardening press, is ideal, as it is for most greenhouse crops and also for bulbs.

Plants in a warm greenhouse will begin to fruit within about seventy days from sowing time and will continue until the end of summer. During the season, each plant will yield a dozen or more fruits which may weigh up to a pound each, though they should be picked before they become too large and exhaust the plant. They are at their best when the skin has a brilliant gloss. Do not allow the plants to lack moisture otherwise the skins of the fruits will split badly.

VARIETIES

Burpee's Hybrid. Disease resistant, it grows 3 ft. tall and does best under glass, producing a continuous supply of oval, medium-sized fruits of dark crimson-purple with a high gloss and a delicious flavour.

Early Beauty. It will come into bearing within sixty-five days and though the fruit is not large, it is prolific and of delicious flavour. The dark purple egg-shaped fruits are held above the ground on plants that grow almost 2 ft. tall.

Long Tom. An early maturing Japanese hybrid, the cucumber-shaped purple-black fruits measure 6-7 in. long and about 2 in. in diameter. A single plant will produce as many as fifty fruits in a season.

CHERIMOYA

One of the exotic fruits of the New World, seed is sown in January, in a propagator in a temperature of 70°F. (21°C.) when it will germinate in about six weeks. Use John Innes sowing compost and sow about a quarter of an inch deep. After germination, lower the temperature to 60°F. (15°C.) and when the plants have formed their first true leaves, transplant to 3 in. pots containing John Innes potting compost and grow on in a temperature of 58°-60°F. (14°-15°C.) syringing occasionally and keeping the compost nicely moist but not wet. Re-pot into larger pots after twelve months and in this size the plants will fruit in another twelve months. The plants are ornamental in their small glossy leaves whilst the fruits are covered in a green scale-like skin and grow 3-4 in. in diameter. They appear in late summer and have pink flesh and a peach-like taste.

CUCUMBER

It is grown up the greenhouse roof, and although heat is necessary for an early crop, French beans may be forced on the bench at the same time. Over a long season, each plant should produce about ten cucumbers, modern varieties being without indigestible qualities.

To have the crop ready by early June, to coincide with the arrival of warm weather, seed is sown, one to a 3-in. pot, early in the new year, but a minimum temperature of 68°F. (20°C.) is necessary and a propagating unit will be the most economic way of raising the plants.

Make up the sowing compost with two parts fibrous loam, one part each peat and sand, and to a bucketful of the mixture add a quarter of an ounce superphosphate of lime to encourage root action. Mix it well in. The seed is planted 1 in. deep on its side. Water in and raise the temperature to 75°F. (24°C.) to hasten germination.

In three weeks, the seedlings will be large enough to move to 60-size pots. These will contain a compost made up of fibrous loam, peat, decayed manure and sand in equal parts by bulk. Cucumbers require an 'open' compost, not too compact. The plants are now grown-on in the greenhouse in a temperature of 68°F. (20°C.) keeping the compost comfortably moist.

By mid-March the plants will be ready to move to larger pots containing a similar compost in which they will fruit.

Place 3 ft. apart and as the plants make growth, fasten to wires stretched across the greenhouse roof. These are fixed at intervals of 12 in. It is necessary to maintain a moist atmosphere by frequent syringing of the plants and damping-down the house. Ventilation may not be needed until the fruits have begun to form and then only on mild days. Allow the main stem to grow up the roof but 'stop' (pinch out) the laterals at the second leaf. These are the side shoots and it is here that the fruits are formed. Any flowers which appear on the main stem are removed. Give the plants a top dressing of decayed manure in June and feed with liquid manure once every three weeks from then onwards. This will greatly increase the size and quality of the fruits.

DISEASES

Gummosis. It is the Cladosporium disease of cucumbers, appearing on the young fruits, from which an unpleasant-smelling liquid exudes. Young fruits often fall before reaching an appreciable size. Dusting the plants with flowers of sulphur at fortnightly intervals from planting time will usually prevent an outbreak, or spraying with colloidal sulphur will give control where the disease occurs.

Leaf Blotch. It attacks the leaves of cucumber and melon, first as brownish spots, later spreading to cover the whole leaf with brown markings. Control is difficult and where the disease occurs grow the resistant variety, Feminex.

VARIETIES

Feminex. As all the flowers are female all will bear fruit. They are long and straight and free from any bitterness whilst being resistant to disease.

Pepimex. An F1 Hybrid, it bears a heavy crop of dark green fruits of medium size and is resistant to disease. The fruit is of mildest flavour.

Topsy. A new hybrid which bears all female flowers whilst the fruits grow about 15 in. long and are especially sweet and juicy.

FRENCH BEANS

French beans are one of the easiest vegetables to force well but a temperature of 65°F. (18°C.) is necessary, combined with constant syringing to keep the plants free from red spider and to help the flowers to set. The new variety Cyrus, slim and stringless, which French cooks use throughout the year is one to grow. If seed is sown in January, the plants will begin to crop at the end of March; or a month later from an early March sowing, so that it will be necessary to maintain a high temperature only in March for quick germination of the seed and during the early life of the plants.

Ten-inch pots are used, containing an open, friable loam and some decayed manure or old mushroom compost, about half and half. Sow four seeds to each, planting them 1 in. deep. Keep the compost nicely moist and as the plants make growth, insert a few twigs around the side of the pot to help them grow upright. During warm, sunny weather admit plenty of fresh air, and damp down the greenhouse floor to encourage a humid atmosphere.

When the first flowers appear, syringe the plants daily, after first dusting the flowers with a camel-hair brush to assist pollination. Water once a week with dilute liquid manure when the first pods have formed to ensure tender beans which should be removed when 5-6 in. long. To allow them to remain too long on the plant will cause them to grow tough and. stringy and reduce the crop.

In order to have enough beans for serving to several people, sow at least ten pots for which half a pint of seed will be required.

French beans may also be sown in pots in a frame early in April, when they will begin to crop fully a month before those from outdoor plantings and will be welcome when vegetables are scarce. The two best varieties for growing under glass are Canadian Wonder and Masterpiece, and the round stringless beans Sprite and Cyrus.

VARIETIES

Canadian Wonder. An old favourite but the best variety for growing in heat. It is early and prolific and bears long stringless pods of excellent flavour.

Cyrus. A Continental variety which crops heavily under glass, the beans being round and of pencil thickness.

Masterpiece. Good indoors and in the open, cropping heavily, the long green pods being succulent and of delicate flavour.

Sprite. A round stringless bean as grown on the Continent, the long dark pods being extremely tender.

MELON

Melons are divided into two groups: (a) those which crop better in a warm greenhouse, e.g., Sutton's Superlative and Emerald Gem, and (b) those which crop equally well in a frame or in a cold greenhouse. These are the cantaloup melons such as Sweetheart and Charantais, grown in large numbers in France and Italy, also in Israel and the Lebanon for export to Britain, whilst being much appreciated in the warm climate of the Mediterranean for their abundance of juice. In Britain, melons are almost a luxury yet there is nothing difficult in their culture.

Whether growing in a heated greenhouse or in a frame, seed is sown in February in small pots since, like cucumbers, they resent root disturbance. A brisk temperature of 65°F. (18°C.) is necessary for their germination so that a propagating unit should be used. For a compost, use John Innes and give little water until germination. When the pots are full of roots, move to a larger size in which will be a friable sandy loam into which has been mixed a sprinkling of bone flour and sulphate of potash. By mid-April, if grown-on in a temperature of 58°-60°F. (14°-15°C.), the plants will be ready to move to larger pots in which they will fruit; or deep boxes may be used, filled with equal parts loam and decayed manure into which has been mixed a handful of bone meal and hoof and horn meal to each pot.

Place the pots (or boxes) close to the glass on the staging and train the plants over the roof of the house; or if growing in a frame, plant in May, keeping the frame closed at night until early June. When the plants are 8 in. high, nip out the tops and grow-on two strong lateral shoots. These in turn are pinched back to about 12 in. and grown-on, tying the shoots to strong wires stretched across the roof of the greenhouse.

Melons bear male and female flowers on the same plant and are pollinated by hand. Dust each flower regularly with a camel-hair brush or remove a male flower and turn back the petals to expose the bunch of stamens. These are inserted into the female (which is the one with a swelling at the base) and will pollinate the stigma. One male will fertilize four or five females and they must all be pollinated together so that the melons will form at the same time.

Melons like plenty of sunlight so do not shade the glass as for tomatoes. They need ample supplies of moisture at the roots, otherwise they will grow small and lack juice. At the same time, watering when not necessary may cause an attack of root rot, causing the plants to die.

So that the plants have room to develop, allow 2 ft. between each when in the greenhouse and permit only four fruits to develop on each plant. Maintain a humid atmosphere during sunny weather by damping down the house and syringing frequently.

After pollination the flowers will wither and the young melons begin to form. At this time, to enable the plant to concentrate its energies on the swelling of the melons, the fruit-bearing shoots are stopped at the second leaf. This will also prevent the plants making excess leaf which would deprive them of sunlight and hinder ripening.

When about grapefruit size, the melons should be strung up in nets fastened to the wires which will take the weight of the fruits until they are ripe. Do not remove the melons too soon; wait until they have reached the size of a small football and have begun to part from the stem. A melon is ready for eating when, held in the hands, it gives slightly at the base when pressed with the thumbs. If no impression is made, place the melons in a box lined with cotton wool and leave in a warm room for several days to ripen.

GREENHOUSE VARIETIES

Crenshaw. An F1 Hybrid, it matures just after Sweetheart when the smooth skin turns pale green and the salmon flesh is sweet and juicy. Allow an hour in the refrigerator before serving. Deep freezing also brings out the flavour.

Emerald Gem. The medium-sized fruits are dark green and netted with grey markings whilst the flesh, which is sweet and juicy, is also green.

Ha-Ogen. The famous melon of Israel, now available in Britain for the first time. It differs from others in that the plants yield up to twenty fruits of the size of a large grapefruit with orange-yellow skins and greenish white flesh of excellent flavour.

Superlative. A Sutton's introduction, the fruits are handsomely netted and, when ripe, the yellow flesh turns almost scarlet.

FRAME VARIETIES

Charantais. A superb frame melon, it bears heavy crops in an average summer, the fruits having thick orange flesh of outstanding flavour.

Golden Crispy The frame counterpart of the greenhouse Ha-Ogen, it will bear up to ten fruits per plant, each weighing one pound or more, with a thin golden skin and greenish flesh which is sweet and juicy.

Sweetheart. The earliest outdoor melon to mature, it will ripen in southern England without glass protection, its grey-green fruits having salmon-orange flesh of excellent flavour.

OKRA

This interesting vegetable is little known in England but in the U.S.A. is widely grown. With its spiny skin it resembles a ridge cucumber; it is 9 in. long and about 1 in. in diameter, terminating in a point. It is also known as Okro and Gumbo and imparts its own delicious flavour to soups and stews, whilst it may also be peeled and sliced and served as a vegetable with meats. The pods or fruits are used before they become too large, as the crop will be reduced if they are left too long.

Seed is sown in small pots in gentle heat in March, John Innes sowing compost being suitable. Soon after germination, transfer the plants, with the soil ball intact, to larger pots containing John Innes potting compost and again to 10-in. pots in about three weeks' time. Here, the compost should be of two parts loam and one part each sand and decayed manure. As the weather becomes warmer, water copiously and syringe the plants to keep them free from red spider. Syringing will also help the fruit to set. The plants grow up to 4 ft. in height, about the same as tomatoes with which they may be grown, and they will require staking.

The first pods will be ready to remove early in August, and if the plants are regularly looked over and the pods removed before they grow too large, they will yield a long succession of fruits until the house is cleared at the end of October. Watering once a week with dilute liquid manure will greatly increase the yield and quality.

VARIETIES

Clemson Spineless. It is free of spines, and the dark green fruits must be removed when 8-9 in. long, though will be more tender if picked when smaller.

Dwarf Green Longpod. Making a short bushy plant 2 ft. tall, it bears a profusion of dark green pods 6-7 in. long, covered in small spines and deeply ribbed.

This variety may be grown outdoors in Britain south of the Thames. Plant 18 in. apart early in June and in a rich soil. Keep the plants well watered in dry weather.

PEPPERS

There are two groups – the Sweet Peppers, *Capsicum annum* and the Hot, *C. baccatum* (the Cayenne peppers), but it is the former that are most wanted for growing in the home greenhouse. Seed is sown early in March in small pots containing John Innes compost in a temperature of 60°F. (16°C.), or it may be sown in boxes and the seedlings transplanted to small pots when large enough to handle. Grow-on in a similar temperature, syringing the plants frequently to prevent an outbreak of red spider and, about 1 May, move to larger pots containing a compost made up of equal parts of fibrous loam, decayed manure and coarse sand. Discontinue artificial heat in early May and, towards the end of the month, move to larger pots containing a compost similar to that recommended for the earlier potting. Give the plants a daily syringe and never allow the compost to dry out. Weekly applications of dilute liquid manure will enhance the quality of the fruits. When removing the ripe fruit, handle carefully for the skins bruise easily.

To guard against blossom-end rot which is caused by physiological disturbance and allows the fruit to become infected by bacteria, never expose the plants to draughts when growing under glass, especially when the fruit has set.

VARIETIES

Canape (Sweet). An F1 Hybrid cross between a Japanese mosaic-resistant line and an American variety. Early to mature, it shows typical hybrid vigour through all stages of its growth. The plants grow 30 in. tall with dark green leaves and it crops heavily. The fruits are about 2 in. square, three-lobed, with sweet flesh and are quick-maturing.

Early Bountiful. An F1 Hybrid, raised by Sakata & Co. of Japan, this received an Award of Merit from the Royal Horticultural Society. It makes a much-branched plant 18 in. high with dark green foliage and bears fruits 3-4 in. long. It matures quickly and is a prolific cropper.

Fordhook. A heavy cropper, the fruits being almost square and measuring 3-4 in. deep and the same across, with four lobes and smooth skin. The walls are thin, the flesh tender and crisp.

New Ace. An F1 Hybrid possessing the vigour of hybrid varieties, it is early to mature, its lobes being fleshy and sweet whilst it is one of the highest yielding varieties.

Oshkosh. The skin turns to bright canary yellow when ripe whilst the flavour is different from that of other peppers, being sweet and mild. The fruits measure 4 in. long and are about 3 in. across the top.

Slim Pim. It is easy to grow and bears a huge crop of small thin green peppers like gherkins, which should be harvested when no more than 3 in. long. It freezes well.

PESTS AND DISEASES

Fruit Spot. This is caused by the fungus *Colletotrichum nigrum*, spots appearing on the fruits as red depressions. Control by removing infected fruit and spray with weak Bordeaux mixture. The trouble may be eliminated by soaking the seed in cold water for twelve hours, then draining before immersing the seed for five minutes in copper sulphate solution (quarter ounce to one pint of water), drying off and sowing without delay.

Grey Mould. This is *Botrytis cinera* which attacks the stems, leaves, and fruits, causing the appearance of large grey spots. Spraying the plants with Shirlan AG before they come into bloom will give control.

Red Spider. This is the most troublesome pest for plants growing under glass and is most prevalent where conditions are too dry. Frequent syringing of the plants as for tomatoes and cucumbers will usually prevent an outbreak.

TOMATOES

Clean conditions and plenty of light are essential to grow tomatoes well, the most popular of all greenhouse crops. Tobacco smokers should sow anti-virus seed, a safeguard against the introduction of the dreaded tomato mosaic disease which, in a few days, can wipe out an entire house of plants. The seed will have been heat-treated for virus control. It is then tested to ensure that it is free from seed-born infection.

Those with a heated greenhouse can sow the seed in a propagator about mid-January in a temperature of 62°F. (17°C.). After transplanting, grow-on the young plants in the greenhouse in a temperature of 56°F. (14°C.) and this should be maintained during winter.

Where planting in ground beds as is common in a Dutch-light house, work into the soil a quantity of well-decayed manure, then take out several trenches 12 in. deep and 9 in. wide. Into the trenches place upright moist wheat straw to a depth of 6 in. Cover it with a layer of soil and allow three weeks to settle down. Then fill in the trenches with the compost and make level with surrounding ground. The straw will allow the maximum amount of air to reach the roots of the plants and this will increase the crop.

Set out the plants 3 ft. apart and keep them moist at the roots and free from draughts but maintaining a buoyant, sweet atmosphere. The plants may be trained up 6 ft. canes or up twine suspended from the roof of the house. Do not remove their growing point until they reach the top or have formed six trusses. The hybrids will carry more.

It may be found more suitable to grow the plants in large pots rather than in ground beds and the plants will be treated in a similar way. For all tomatoes, firm planting is essential and, as the tomato is shallow-rooting, no further cultivation should be done apart from giving the plants a top dressing with decayed manure as the first fruits begin to set.

At an early age, the plants will begin to form side shoots at the point where each leaf joins the main stem. When large enough to handle, the side growths are removed with finger and thumb or with a sharp knife, but take care not to harm the main stem.

As the flowers open, help them to set fruit by dusting them with a camel-hair brush. Also, increase the humidity of the house by damping down on warm days. After the plants have formed their sixth truss, it is necessary to remove the top 3 in. of the main stem so that they will concentrate their energies in the setting and ripening of the trusses – which is usually all they can manage in an average summer. Ensure that the plants do not lack moisture at any stage, for alternating periods of dryness and moisture will cause the fruit to crack. Lack of moisture at the roots will also cause stunting when the plants will be unable to form the normal number of trusses.

As the fruit begins to swell, support the trusses by tying them to the cane with raffia, and remove any side shoots daily. If the plants are in their fruiting quarters by mid-April they will begin to ripen the first fruit by early July. To enable the top trusses to ripen at the end of summer, it will be necessary to defoliate the plants so that all their energies may be directed to this end. This is done gradually and do not begin until early September when the plants will require less water as the warmth of the sun diminishes.

DISEASES

Blight. It is present where brown marks appear on the leaves, and if not checked it will cause the leaves to turn brown and die. Spray with weak Bordeaux mixture, made by dissolving four ounces copper sulphate and three ounces of slaked lime in two gallons of water.

Cladosporium. This is the name of the disease (also known as leaf mould) which attacks the leaves causing them to be covered in yellowish-brown mould. If unchecked, it will attack the calyx of the fruit, then the fruit itself. If experienced, plant mould-resistant varieties, but to control, spray the plants (preferably as routine) with mildew specific shortly after planting and every three weeks afterwards.

Greenback. A disorder rather than a disease whereby the fruits remain green around the top and refuse to ripen however warm the sun. Lack of potash in the soil is possibly the chief cause but if experienced, grow immune varieties.

Mosaic. A destructive virus disease usually introduced to indoor tomatoes by tobacco smokers. Guard against this as there is no cure. Remove and burn infected plants and, if a smoker, wash the hands before entering the greenhouse.

VARIETIES

Alicante. A high-yielding variety from Suttons and ripening free from greenback. The tomatoes are of even size and produced in long trusses.

Amberley Cross. Raised at the Glasshouse Research Institute, it is the earliest variety to ripen in a warm greenhouse and shows no greenback. It requires plenty of room to develop for although setting good first trusses, it grows and crops with vigour until late autumn.

Astra. Unusual in that the large trusses grow at one side of the plant only. It crops well in a cold or heated greenhouse whilst the large fleshy fruits have good flavour.

Craigella. It has the reliable Ailsa Craig as a parent and crops as heavily, being virtually free from greenback. It ripens early, the trusses being borne right to the top of the plants and whilst the fruits are of medium size, they are of brightest scarlet.

Dobie's Peach. The large trusses number up to twenty or more fruits even in shape and of yellowish-orange colouring, with very low acid content, making it one of the best for eating raw.

Kelvedon Cross. It crops well in a cold and a heated greenhouse, the trusses being closely spaced, the globular fruits ripening early and with no trace of greenback.

M.M. A hybrid, similar to Moneymaker but bearing larger trusses. The well-coloured fruit is without greenback whilst the plant is resistant to cladosporium. It also does well in a cold greenhouse.

Moneymaker. An old favourite, still outstanding for a cold or only slightly heated greenhouse. It bears large trusses of evenly-sized fruits of excellent colour and fine flavour. It does equally well outdoors.

Pagham Cross. A variety for smokers for it yields heavily and is immune to mosaic. Making a big leafy plant, it is is also resistant to cladosporium and crops for at least five months.

Red Ensign. It is recommended for the amateur with little experience of tomato growing, for it sets its first truss well. It also comes quickly into bearing and is equally good in a cold or heated greenhouse. From an early sowing it will begin cropping about mid-June. It is resistant to cladosporium and is free from greenback.

One of nature's secrets given to me by Mr. Keith Sangster of the famous seed firm of Thompson & Morgan of Ipswich is that in their native South America, tomatoes are known to grow better and crop heavier if French or African marigolds are growing with or near them. This may be worth trying whether growing indoors or outside. They also tend to keep white fly from tomatoes.

YELLOW GUAVA

It may be grown in a garden-room or in a comfortably warm living-room and is most decorative with its pointed glossy dark green leaves and bright yellow skinned fruits like small oranges, and which have a deep pink flesh. They are eaten as a dessert fruit after meals and are rich in vitamin C.

This is an easy plant to grow and should be raised in a propagator but can be grown-on in a light, airy room for it prefers a dry atmosphere and just enough moisture at its roots to keep it alive.

Germination is similar in all respects to the cherimoya and it will also fruit in about two years after the seed is sown. It grows 3-4 ft. tall and will fruit almost continuously.

CHAPTER EIGHT

FOOD FROM A FRAME

The most valuable asset a town gardener can possess is a frame, especially if it can be heated. It can then be kept in use the whole year round. In winter it will support lettuce and other salad crops. If the frame has two lights (i.e., it is a double frame, a light being sheets of glass held together by laths) onion and leek plants, celery and celeriac, all crops which require a long season to come to maturity, can be sown in the new year, as can tomatoes, cucumbers and melons which will be grown-on in the frame to bear fruit when the frame is cleared of other plants. An early crop of cauliflowers can be raised for planting out early in April to mature in June; and French and runner beans can be sown in boxes to plant out at the end of May.

If the frame cannot be heated, sowing will be delayed, but a cold frame is almost as useful. It will be available for hardening-off plants raised in a heated greenhouse which need gradual acclimatization to outdoor temperatures before they are planted out. Afterwards, the frame can be used for a crop of marrows, tomatoes or cucumbers which have been raised in a propagator and grown-on in a warm greenhouse; or if this is not possible, the plants may be obtained from a specialist grower or garden shop ready to plant in the frame early in April. If the frame is kept closed for most of the time in April and is covered with sacking or matting at night to exclude hard frost, an early crop may be expected, the first tomatoes being ready by the end of June, fully a month before outdoor plants will have ripened their first fruits.

Those plants which require a long season to develop, e.g.

onions and leeks, can be sown in a cold frame early in autumn when it is cleared of tomatoes and marrows. Under another light, a hardy winter lettuce such as Continuity or All the Year Round may be grown-on to mature in the new year and if a sowing of radishes is made in autumn, these will be ready at the same time. Sow spring onions in the garden in August to mature with the radishes – they will stand a severe winter without protection.

Early in April, year-old strawberry plants may be lifted and potted and placed in a cold frame to fruit early in June, before the outdoor plants begin to bear their crop. The autumn-fruiting varieties, so long appreciated on the Continent and now being more widely grown in Britain, may be planted in frames in pots when the tomatoes and cucumbers are removed in September; they will continue to crop almost until Christmas and are much appreciated at this time. After they have finished fruiting, plant them out in March and remove the first flowers which appear in June, for it is not until autumn that their blossom is wanted to form fruit.

A cold frame has other uses too. It can be used to raise autumn-sown sweet peas which are wintered under glass and, after hardening, are planted out in April; summer bedding plants such as antirrhinums, ageratum and lobelia, the seed being sown the previous summer and the plants treated as biennials; and all manner of cuttings, of pinks and chrysanthemums, of shrubs and herbaceous plants, alpines and miniature roses.

MAKES AND SIZES OF FRAMES

There are many ways of making a frame and there are several on the market already made up to correct specifications, but it is not advisable to have the lights more than 4 ft. by 3 ft. in size, otherwise they are difficult to lift when opening and closing the frame. The frame made by BEC Limited of Winchester is neatly constructed and efficient. Approximately 40 in. by 30 in. in size, it is made of ICI's propathene, the sides being assembled by bolting them together. The light consists of twin panes of glass. The frame can be assembled anywhere, in the sunny corner of a courtyard over an asphalt or concrete surface; on a terrace or verandah; or in the garden. It is not necessary to have the frame over a soil base for many crops can be raised in boxes or pots in which they spend their whole life, their crops giving complete satisfaction.

The Crittall-Hope frames are made of galvanized aluminium treated by the hot-dip process to give lasting protection against rust and decay. A single frame is 4 ft. long by 2 ft. 6 in. wide and is 18 in. high at the back, 14 in. at the front. Extensions can be added. The frame opens by gently sliding the light forward so that one reaches inside the frame from the back. The Span roof frame, which is two frames back to back, provides double the space under glass.

A home-made frame may be constructed of wood, the sides made with a gentle slope of no more than 3 in. so that the back boards will be 15 in. high and the front 12 in., and made to take a light 4 ft. by 3 ft. This may also be made of wood and painted white or green to match the frame so that wherever it is sited, it will not in any way be unsightly.

As an alternative to glass, transparent polythene sheeting may be used for the lights, but in this case it is advisable to stretch wires across the top and bottom of the light, fastened to hooks on either side of the frame, to hold the light secure in windy weather.

The frame is constructed by cutting the timber so that the back and front lengths are 2 in. longer than the lights and the sides will fit inside the two ends, which are held in place by metal angle-pieces screwed on to the wood at top and bottom of each of the four corners.

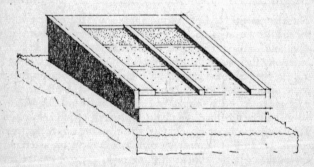

For the garden, where neatness of construction may not be so important, a simple frame can be constructed from old railway sleepers, one placed on top of another so that the frame will be about 9 in. deep. Full length sleepers can be used for the back and front and two lights made to the required dimensions, but the side sleepers will need to be cut so that they will fit inside those at the back and front.

Sleepers can be placed over a base of asphalt or cement for they will be held in place by their own weight, and if they are unsightly, they can be surrounded with 'window' boxes made to the same dimensions in length and about 9 in. wide. The boxes can also be used to grow food crops.

Where a frame is to be made over a soil base, it may be constructed from boards, held in position by wooden stakes driven well into the ground at each corner and to which the boards are nailed. Transparent polythene sheeting may be used for the lights, tacking it onto the frames which can be inexpensively made from builders' laths. Claritex is a new material which has a high reputation for toughness and light transmission.

THE USE OF A HOTBED

A frame of the above description can be erected over a hotbed for early crops where the electric supply is not available. When horse manure was plentiful, a hotbed was made by composting a load of manure until, by bacterial action, it was generating considerable heat. A hole, of the dimensions of the frame and 6-8 in. deep was made by excavating the soil and into it the manure was placed, treading it well down to conserve the heat. Then the frame was put in place and the hotbed covered with a 2 in. layer of sifted loam. Into this, seed would be sown or plants set out.

A hotbed is made up in February and cauliflower and broccoli should be sown immediately for early cropping outdoors, whilst early turnips and carrots can be obtained by sowing seed over the hotbed about 1 March and keeping the frame closed. The thinnings will be used first, while the remaining plants will be tender and sweet and much appreciated when ready to use at the end of April. Remember to sow quick maturing varieties. At this time, tomatoes, marrows and melons for growing-on in the frame can be sown. Dwarf and runner beans can be sown in boxes to plant out in May; also celery, leeks and onions, which require a long season to mature. After these have been planted out when the soil is in a friable condition, the frames are used for hardening those plants raised in a warm greenhouse, the hotbed having been removed for further use on the land.

Though riding schools and a few army barracks where horses are kept will mostly be situated near a town, manure is in such short supply that one may have to compost a bale or two of straw, obtainable from farms or agricultural merchants. First shake out the straw in a corner formed by two walls, or in an area specially constructed of corrugated sheeting held in place by wooden stakes, and thoroughly soak it. Then, as it is built up into a heap, sprinkle a composting agent such as Adco over a 9 in. layer of straw and repeat the process until all the straw is used up. Cover the top with old sacking and allow it to stand for a week whilst it heats up. Then turn the heap, shaking out the straw and the agent so that it is well mixed in. Give more water if the straw appears too dry and leave the heap another week, by which time it will have turned a rich brown colour and will reach a temperature of up to 100°F. (38°C.). A better compost will be obtained if a small quantity of poultry manure or droppings from a pigeon loft can be mixed in. If this has been stored dry, it will be quite clean to handle. A well made hotbed should be dark brown and have a rich aroma. It should also be of the right moisture content to allow for treading to conserve the heat without becoming too compact, which occurs if there is excess moisture and allows the bed to lose its heat.

Where an electric supply is available, soil warming for seed germination and for early salads and other crops, may be inexpensively obtained by the use of warming wires and cables, placed 12 in. below the surface. A transformer unit which reduces the mains supply to a safe low voltage is used to heat a plastic-covered galvanized wire placed under a bed of soil or sand. Where there is danger of cultivation disturbance, cables should be used instead of wires.

To make an electric hotbed, a minimum load of 6 watts per sq. ft. of bed is allowed and the current is switched on, generally at night, for a long enough period to burn 70 watts per sq. ft. in every twenty-four hours. Soil retains its temperature for a considerable time when heated and even after turning off the heater, there will be no rapid fall in temperature as with air heating. The use of soil-warming wires in a heated greenhouse will enable the air temperature to be reduced to a minimum without harm to the plants for they will be kept growing by the gentle bottom heat.

A sand propagating frame may be made in a cold greenhouse by using low voltage warming wires. A wooden box is made of 9 in. boards, the base being covered with thick felt. Over this is placed a 2 in. layer of washed sand, then the warming wires, with a further 3 in. layer of sand on which the seed boxes or pots will stand. Eight watts per sq. ft. of sand should be allowed and a soil thermostat is necessary to control the temperature of the bed.

THE VALUE OF CLOCHES

As an alternative to a frame, use barn-type or tent cloches to bring on early crops. The Chase barn cloche has for long maintained a reputation for reliability. They are 24 in. long by 23 in. wide when assembled and are 12 in. at the highest point, so that they remain in position over bush tomato plants until such time as they fill the entire cloche with foliage and the fruit is beginning to ripen. The glass cloches are held together by galvanized wires which do not rust and are sold in packs of eight for quick assembly, together with end shields to exclude draught. The tent cloche is only 15 in. wide and 10 in. high so is suitable for a double row of lettuce and other salad crops.

The barn cloche is the most useful for it will take a double row of French beans until they have finished cropping; also the dwarf runner bean, Hammond's Early, which grows only 9 in. high and sends out its stems in all directions and which may be trained beneath the cloches. Marrows, melons and frame cucumbers can be trained under the cloches and they can be used to cover a double row of strawberry plants which will have been planted to the dimensions of the cloches. To keep them constantly employed they can be used to cover early strawberries or French beans, then used for early bush tomatoes, followed by autumn-fruiting strawberries and then winter lettuce. They may also be used in the early new year to place over a hotbed on which has been sown early maturing carrots or turnips.

A simple way of making one's own cloches is to have the glass sheets cut to size by a hardware merchant or plumber and to hold them in position with the Russell cloche holders. These are made of high quality durable rubber and hold the glass rigid. There is less breakage of the glass, and the rubber is not affected by the weather. The Rumsey cloche clip, recently on the market, is also highly efficient.

A virtually unbreakable giant cloche made with Claritex, a product of British Celanese, held in position by galvanized steel hoops is wide enough to take three rows of lettuce. The cloche is frost-proof and may be compactly stored.

Using steel hoops for the shape, a long tunnel cloche may be made up from ICI's PVC sheeting. These long cloches are useful for covering rows of seedlings to protect them from frost in the early spring, whilst they are suitable for lettuce and other salad crops.

For those who have to be away from home for long hours, the Marmax self-watering cloche is recommended. It is 25 in. long and 12 in. wide, and has a specially shaped top with four rows of apertures which allow the rain to enter and water the plants beneath.

The unique Rainmaker hose, manufactured by G. Pine Limited of Chichester, is also a valuable help to efficient watering. Made from PVC it is really three hoses in one, of which one has specially designed slits from which issues a heavy mist which keeps the plants drenched in moisture, thus promoting rapid growth. By controlling the supply from the tap, the width of irrigation can be varied from 6 in. to 3 ft. The hose may be laid along a border or trough made by a low wall in which fruit or vegetables are growing. Its use goes far to eliminate the need to stand for hours watering with an ordinary hose, whilst it may also be used to water lawns and tennis courts.

Food Plants for Frames and Cloches

The plants mostly grown in a frame or beneath cloches will be those needing protection from frost and cold winds during early summer or protection from the cold in winter. The use of glass or

PVC sheeting to cover plants will greatly increase the total quantity of food a garden can produce in any year. Here is a cropping programme for a cold frame:

Fruit or Vegetable	Sow	To plant in frame or under cloches	Maturing
Aubergine	January	Early May	August
Bean, dwarf	Early March	Early April	June-July
Bean, runner	Early March	Early May	August-September
Carrot	Early March	—	May-June
Cauliflower	March	Early April	June-July
Cucumber	Early March	Early May	July-August
Lettuce (autumn)	July	Early September	November-December
Lettuce (winter)	August	October	January-March
Marrow	February	Early April	July
Melon	Early March	Early May	June-July
Radish	Early March	—	May
Strawberry	Cover early April	—	June
Strawberry (autumn fruiting)	Cover late August	—	September-October
Tomato (bush)	Early March	Early May	July-August
Turnip	Early March		May-June

CARROT

When sown over a mild hotbed in February, the roots will be ready for use early in May, a time of scarcity in vegetables. If a frame is not available, a sowing may be made over a hotbed in a sheltered, sunny corner in early March, when the roots will be ready towards the end of May.

The seed is best sown broadcast into a finely-screened soil, radishes being sown at the same time for an early crop, for they will be removed before the carrots mature. If the carrot seedlings are overcrowded they must be thinned, although if used when young they will not need as much space to mature in as will maincrop varieties. The bed should be kept comfortably moist, the frames being closed during cold weather, with as much air as possible being admitted when milder.

VARIETIES

Amsterdam Forcing. Excellent for frames, for the plants make little foliage whilst the cylindrical roots are free of core.

Early Nantes. For early forcing this is one of the best. It has a long stump root, almost free of any core. The flavour is mild and sweet, and rich in carotene.

Kurna. The short, stumpy carrots grow uniform and mature quickly. When cooked, they are sweet and tender and equally so when grated raw into a winter salad.

Paris Forcing. Possibly the best all-round carrot, bearing bright orange roots the size of a tennis ball. It forces well and may be sown for succession throughout the year.

CUCUMBER

What are known as 'frame' cucumbers may be grown where a cold frame or barn-type cloches are available. Where there is no glass then grow the 'ridge' varieties to have summer cucumbers. These are the hardiest of all, whilst those for frames are also suitable for growing in a heated greenhouse. The frame varieties are quite the equal of greenhouse cucumbers for flavour and tenderness and they are just as prolific and easily grown. They will grow in a well-manured bed of soil, although growing over a gentle hotbed will bring on an earlier crop and give fruit for at least another month.

Sowing the Seed

Make up the hotbed at the end of March, placing the compost 18 in. deep in the frames and cover with 6 in. of soil. When the temperature has fallen to below 80°F. (27°C.), sow the seed. Cucumbers are intolerant of root disturbance, so always sow the seed where the plants are to grow rather than in pots. If there are two lights, the frame will accommodate three plants, two seeds being sown close together in three parts of the frame, the stronger plant in each group being retained. If fresh manure is not available, then the soil should be enriched to a depth of 8 in. with well-decayed manure.

Seed is sown in damp soil early in April and, being slower to germinate owing to lack of bottom heat, the plants will begin to fruit about a month later.

After sowing, cover with the lights and place sacking over them at night to retain as much heat as possible. Keep the frames closed to maintain a warm, humid atmosphere until the seed has germinated. If the temperature of the frame falls due to the hotbed losing heat, heap some soil around the frame boards to give additional warmth.

Keep the plants moist but not wet, and use slightly warm water for spraying and watering. Until the end of May, any damping down done on warm days should be done before mid-day, so that the moisture will dry off the plants before the cooler temperature of night. Regular spraying is necessary to keep down red spider, and in any case, cucumbers require a humid atmosphere and a high degree of moisture at their roots. If the plants are too dry they will drop their fruits.

Bringing on the Crop

As the plants grow, space out the shoots and peg them down so that each has room to develop. When they have formed the second leaf the laterals should be stopped, the sub-laterals being grown-on, and if the frame becomes too crowded, remove excess growth altogether. Never allow the fruits to grow too large, for they will not only lose texture and flavour, but will crowd the frames, at the same time taking too much out of the plants. It is better to have a lot of smaller fruits over a longer period. Ventilate freely whenever the day is warm.

The flowers will set their own fruit but before the frame becomes too filled with plant growth, give the plants a light top dressing, using finely-sifted loam to which has been added some peat and a little decayed manure. This will provide the surface roots with nourishment, and will act as a mulch in keeping the roots moist.

If when the first fruits have begun to form, the plants are watered every ten days with liquid manure, this will also increase the vigour of the plants and produce a heavier crop. As the fruits have a tendency to decay if they come into contact with the soil, each should be placed on a piece of wood (not glass, as it tends to hold moisture) until the fruit is removed.

Growing under Cloches

Cucumbers may be grown under barn cloches. Mark out the ground to the width of the glass and into it dig some decayed manure to a depth of 10 in. Do this in March and place the glass in position a full week before the seeds are sown 4 ft. apart at the end of April. The plants, from the seedling stage, should be kept moist at the roots, and a humid atmosphere maintained exactly the same as when growing in frames by placing a sheet of glass at each end of the row of cloches.

Stop the plants at the fourth leaf, two laterals only being allowed to develop, which in turn are stopped at the fifth leaf. A mulch of peat and soil given in June and regular syringing during hot weather will ensure plenty of fruit over a long period. If the plants make too much foliage, some defoliation can be done by degrees but this must not be excessive.

VARIETIES

Burpee Hybrid. It bears an immense crop of thick, short fruits about 8 in. long with crisp flesh of good flavour.

Butcher's Disease-Resisting. An old variety which is hardy and vigorous and is recommended for northern gardens.

Conqueror. For a frame especially if given a hotbed, it has no equal in its cropping, the dark green fruits being of even shape. Can be grown in the north with confidence.

Every Day. Valuable in that it will set its fruit in a sunless summer. The fruits have a smooth dark green skin and are mild and juicy.

Patio Pik. Likely to become widely planted in frames for it makes a compact plant and over a hotbed will begin fruiting mid-June. In a season, one plant will bear up to thirty fruits which should be harvested when 6-7 in. long.

LETTUCE

No crop does better in a frame, and where heated it will be possible to enjoy this salad all the year round, seed being sown at fortnightly intervals. Seed can be sown under cloches or in boxes in a frame late in autumn when there will be lettuce to cut from early spring. By sowing outdoors at fortnightly intervals, there will be supplies from mid-summer until Christmas. Plants for cutting in winter should be in their frame (or under cloches) by early October but in the warmer parts of Britain, lettuce may be grown entirely in the open all the year round.

When preparing the soil in a frame, work in some old mushroom-bed compost or a little peat and decayed manure. Used hops from a brewery will be of value.

Sow the seed thinly and transplant the seedlings to the frame or cloches when large enough to handle To provide a succession, the amateur should sow a pinch of seed every month throughout the year so that there will be a continuous supply and never too many plants. But remember to sow the varieties for each season at the right time. Winter lettuce should not be grown in summer for they would run to seed too quickly, nor will summer lettuce heart well in winter.

Growers living in an exposed area will sow under glass early August for cutting from November until spring, or for early spring maturing in a favourable climate. Cold does not worry lettuce but damp, foggy weather causes it to damp off. For early summer, seed is sown under glass in February, for planting out early April.

With lettuce it is important to keep the plants growing from the moment the seed is sown, watering during periods of drought, but keeping the plants under glass as dry as possible through winter. Water only the soil and not the plants. Lettuce under glass will damp-off if not kept as dry and as well ventilated as possible through winter. To prevent mildew, dust the plants with sulphur every fortnight and raise the frame light on sunny days.

Give them no artificial nitrogen otherwise they will not heart well and in winter will tend to be soft, so falling a victim to mildew or botrytis. The plants can be used as soon as they begin to heart so as not to have them ready all together.

VARIETIES FOR GROWING IN A FRAME OR UNDER CLOCHES:

French Frame. Very quick to mature, making a much-appreciated contribution to a Christmas salad. The leaves are pale green.

Kwick. A cabbage-type lettuce for sowing in early autumn to mature over winter. It hearts quickly, forming a large head of pale green, and makes crisp eating.

Masterpiece. Maturing in early spring, the leaves are almost free from the usual red tinge of frame lettuce.

Tom Thumb. This lettuce cannot be too highly praised. It may be sown and used throughout the year and, in exposed gardens, wintered under cloches. It makes a compact, dark green head, the leaves being very crisp and icy cool.

STRAWBERRIES

Strawberries are a satisfactory crop to grow in frames or under cloches. Under glass the fruit will be clean and no splash protection need be given, but unless correctly ventilated the plants may suffer from mildew and the fruits from botrytis, a disease which causes them to decay. To ripen fruit under glass calls for a degree of skill, and by covering the plants too soon they will not have had a sufficient time to recover from the previous year's fruiting. When winter comes the strawberry plant, like the grower himself, is ready for a rest, and so should be given a period of cold to become revitalized. However early a crop is desired, no plants should be covered before early March after having first been given a dressing with potash. This is necessary to build up a 'hard' mildew-resistant plant. For the same reason grow mildew-resistant varieties under glass culture, and those which do not make an excess of leaf. But strawberries are hardy plants, and demand the maximum of ventilation, and so the less foliage the plants make the better, so that there will be plenty of air about them.

It will be necessary to decide upon the type of glass to be used before planting, for it is essential to be able to cover the maximum number of plants to make the glass economical. Dutch or ordinary garden lights may be supported on 9 in. boards, or on old railway sleepers. Under lights, the plants should be 12 in. apart each way, so that it may be possible to plant four rows of a compact variety.

Make up the beds in spring and do not let the plants bear fruit that summer. They need as long a period of growth as possible if they are to bear fruit under glass the following year. The soil must be deeply worked and enriched, and only top-quality plants should be used. Where barn-type cloches are used, make a double row 9 in. apart, allowing 18 in. in the rows. A single row with the plants 15 in. apart may be covered with tent cloches. Cloches may be used again in autumn to cover the late fruiting strawberries. Late July or early August is often a time of heavy rain and cloches may also be used to protect the ripening fruit of a late variety, such as Cambridge Rearguard, during a period of adverse weather.

These varieties crop well under glass:

Cambridge Aristocrat	Cambridge Rival
Cambridge Premier	Cambridge Vigour
Cambridge Regent	Royal Sovereign

All these varieties are early maturing, resistant to mildew, and are of compact habit. Where growing under cloches, make the rows from north to south to make for even ripening of the fruit.

Covering the Fruit

Before covering the plants give them a thorough soaking, especially after hard frost which leaves the soil dry and powdery. Then dust the plants with flowers of sulphur to guard against mildew, repeating at fortnightly intervals. By late March the sun's rays will be warmer, and on suitable occasions ventilation should be given during the daytime though not when a cold wind is blowing. In an exposed position, take care to ensure that the lights are prevented from being blown about and broken, holding them in position by strong telephone wire stretched over the glass.

When ventilating the plants they will often need a soaking, though on mild, moist April days the coverings may be left off for several hours to obtain moisture naturally. The plants will then be coming into bloom, and this will help with their fertilization. Moisture should be given before noon to enable the surplus to dry off the flower trusses before nightfall. But until the end of March it is not advisable to give too much water, otherwise hard night frosts may damage the plants as they make new foliage. On mild days, the glass protection should be removed during the day, up to the time when the fruit begins to ripen. At this stage the glass is kept in place to give protection and hasten ripening so that picking may commence early in May. There is little demand for the fruit until then, and it is during the last weeks of May and in early June, when the weather becomes warmer and before the first of the outdoor fruit is ripe, that strawberries under glass are most appreciated.

Both first- and second-year plants may be covered but, to build up a vigorous growth for second year cloching, they must be heavily mulched as soon as fruiting has ended, and fed with dilute manure water in summer. After covering for two years, it is advisable to destroy the plants and begin again.

VARIETIES

Cambridge Premier. Resistant to mildew it crops heavily under cloches, making a compact plant. The large, bright-orange, wedge-shaped fruit is firm and freezes well but if this variety has a fault, it is that the tip of the berry may remain green when the rest has ripened.

Cambridge Profusion. It is early and useful for cloching as it makes little foliage, whilst it is resistant to mildew. The round crimson berries are of good flavour.

Cambridge Regent. It is possibly the best early strawberry outdoors and under glass in the north for its blossom is highly resistant to frost though mildew may be troublesome in a damp, humid spring. The large, orange-scarlet wedge-shaped fruits possess good texture and quality.

Cambridge Vigour. At East Malling Research Station trials, it gave the heaviest crops, bearing almost double the crop of Royal Sovereign, and it has no faults.

Royal Sovereign. Raised by Thomas Laxton and introduced in 1892, its brilliant scarlet, wedge-shaped fruit has never been surpassed for quality and appearance but the virus-free Malling 48 strain should be grown. The fruits have outstanding flavour.

AUTUMN-FRUITING STRAWBERRIES

These may be divided into two types or groups:

(a) Those which bear the whole of their crop during the later part of the year, from August until possibly December; and

(b) Those which yield two distinct flushes of fruit, the first in early summer, the second in late autumn. These are now known as the two-crop strawberries, the remontants, and are especially valuable for the amateur's garden, where space is limited.

Those who have to contend with a lime-laden soil and find that their strawberry plants suffer from serious iron deficiency may be able to enjoy autumn fruit from the late-crop varieties by planting in early spring. The plants are removed at the end of the year after fruiting, and the runners grown-on to fruit the following year. In this way, the plants retain their vigour.

Whilst the true autumn-fruiting varieties may be planted in spring, the two-crop varieties should be planted early in autumn, to enable them to become established before the winter and so bear a crop in the early summer. In this way they occupy the ground only nine months, or they may be grown-on for a second year if given good cultivation. It is also possible to prolong the season of the autumn-fruiting varieties by making a planting both in spring and in autumn. Those planted in autumn are then allowed to set fruit on the first flowering trusses which appear during May. The fruit will be ready about 1 July. Where only late-summer and autumn fruit are required, those planted in spring should be disbudded until 1 June. There will thus be a succession of fruit from midsummer until almost the end of the year.

Those fruiting in autumn are covered with cloches (or frames) in October when they will continue to ripen their fruit until Christmas.

VARIETIES

Charles Simmen. On account of its huge cropping powers and handsome heart-shaped fruit, which is brilliant orange and richly flavoured, this is the finest of all strawberries, but it forms no runners and has to be increased by the slow process of crown division. This is done when new growth commences in April. It crops over a long period and is resistant to botrytis, even in the wettest parts.

Gento. Raised by Herr Hummel of Stuttgart, it begins to crop in June, when the fruits are small, and continues until late October, the fruits increasing in size each week. The large, wedge-shaped berries are red-fleshed and of excellent flavour.

Hampshire Maid. It may be said to bridge the gap between the late-summer and autumn-fruiting varieties, but it is suitable only for light land. It bears sweet, conical fruits on upright trusses over a long period, but will only crop heavily if kept well watered through summer and autumn.

La Sans Rivale. This is the heaviest cropping strawberry, producing up to two pounds per plant if given good culture. It makes little foliage and holds its fruit trusses well above the ground. If the plants are de-blossomed until 1 June it comes into bearing 1 September, reaching a peak at the end of October. The large wedge-shaped fruits are sweet and juicy and of a vivid scarlet colour

St. Claude. It crops over a longer season than any strawberry, maturing its first fruit in August and, in the south, continuing until Christmas. The conical fruits are firm and their size is retained throughout the crop, the skin being glossy and of a dark crimson colour. The plants are highly resistant to botrytis.

TOMATO

If there is not a heated greenhouse available, one must either purchase plants, well hardened off, for planting out early in May in a frame or under cloches, or plants may be raised by sowing the seed over a hotbed in a closed frame early in April.

Make the hotbed 8 in. deep and tread well to conserve heat and moisture. Over the top place a 1 in. covering of sterilized soil or John Innes compost.

Sow the seeds 2 in. apart, just covering with soil. Water in and place the light over the frame. Excessive moisture should not be given, and when germination has taken place, give the seedlings ventilation on all suitable days but cover the frames at night with sacking to exclude frost. When the seedlings have formed their first pair of leaves, move to small pots containing John Innes potting compost.

Late in May, after hardening, set out the plants under cloches or grow-on in the frame. If no cloches are available the plants should remain in the frame until about 1 June before planting in the open. Do not plant out too soon even where glass covering is available, for until June the nights remain cold and there are few insects about to pollinate the first flower trusses. For an early crop it is important that the lower trusses set their fruit.

The bush-type tomatoes may be grown-on in a cold frame, removing the glass altogether by early June, or under cloches. The plants may be grown-on in large pots placed in a frame when the compost should consist of sterilized soil and decayed manure in equal parts. Plants which are growing in large pots where they are to crop will require regular attention with their watering, for the soil will dry out more quickly than in ground beds and bud-drop will result.

Pollinating the Flowers

To assist pollination, carefully brush each flower with a small camel-hair brush, or even with a few hen's feathers tied together. This should take place around midday, when the flowers are open and any moisture has evaporated. Syringing the plants must be withheld until after hand pollinating which is done each day during the early summer.

Bringing on the Crop

Those varieties of dwarf habit such as Pixie, Sleaford Abundance and Tiny Tim, will require neither 'stopping' nor the removal of side shoots. They 'stop' themselves, restricting themselves to forming only a limited number of shoots. Those of taller habit are 'stopped' at the fifth truss, so that they ripen their fruit by late October. The ability of these plants to look after themselves makes them valuable to the gardener with only limited time at his disposal. The orthodox varieties growing to 4 ft. tall, should have the side growths removed with a sharp knife or with the fingers. They grow from the leaf joints.

A light dressing of peat and strawy manure given as a mulch early in July will help to preserve moisture in the soil and keep down annual weeds, thus making hoeing and hand weeding unnecessary, with the danger of damaging the roots if working too near the plants.

Over the mulch place a layer of clean straw to prevent soil splashing, and on which the fruits may rest without coming into contact with the soil. As an aid to ripening a light dressing of sulphate of potash, one ounce per sq. yd., may be given just before the mulch, and from mid-July until mid-September a weekly application of dilute manure water will increase the total weight of fruit and improve its quality.

To assist the fruit to ripen, some defoliation may be done but no leaves should be removed until they have completed their duties in the formation of a strong, healthy plant.

First, cut back the lower leaves. This will prevent an attack of botrytis which may occur with the splashing of the lower leaves with soil through careless watering. It also allows for a free circulation of air, also a safeguard against fungus and so advisable with bush varieties which tend to form more foliage than necessary. It is preferable to cut back the leaves just half-way, as complete defoliation may be too drastic.

If the plants appear to be making too much foliage in a wet, sunless summer, thin out the leaves right to the top when the plant has formed five trusses. Again, it is advisable to cut back only half of each leaf but should the hours of sunshine be above average, it is better not to defoliate for the leaves will protect the plants's roots from strong sunlight.

As the crop draws to its close the sun's warmth becomes weaker, and a certain amount of fruit remains to be ripened. Then more defoliation may be done, for now the plant no longer needs the starches and sugars to produce its crop of fruit.

VARIETIES

French Cross. An F1 Hybrid bush tomato introduced by Suttons, combining the excellent flavour of Continental varieties with uniform shape and ripening, the medium-size round fruits being sweet and juicy.

Gardener's Delight. The tomatoes are not large but are produced in abundance and ripen without any trace of greenback. The flavour is outstanding, being refreshingly tangy and juicy; the fruits being without any trace of hard core.

Pixie. It grows 2 ft. tall yet will carry as many as twenty fruit trusses which will ripen in an average summer. Flavour of the fruit is excellent, and it is sweet and juicy.

Sleaford Abundance. An F1 Hybrid, it grows only 15 in. tall with little foliage, and forms large trusses of well-coloured, medium-sized fruit of excellent flavour which ripen early.

TURNIP

For an early crop, sow over a gentle hotbed towards the end of February, Early Six-Weeks or Tokio Cross. Sow thinly and give plenty of air once the seed has germinated. It is best sown broadcast, thinning to 6 in. apart. Keep the plants well supplied with water when the roots will be ready for pulling by early May. They should be pulled as soon as they reach tennis ball size when they will be sweet and succulent after cooking.

VARIETIES

Early Snowball. Outstanding for early sowing under glass, it makes a shining white globe of mildest flavour.

Early White Six-Weeks. One of the best over a hotbed, maturing in six weeks, the medium-sized roots of purest white being tender and delicately flavoured.

Golden Ball. Delicious when cooked, it makes a small round root with deep yellow flesh and is sweet and juicy.

Tokio Cross. Can be sown throughout the year at monthly intervals, in winter under glass, and it will be ready to lift in about six weeks. The roots, with their delicate flavour, are pure white.

VEGETABLE MARROW

Courgettes and small marrows are now very popular but all marrows need planting in full sun and where they may be sheltered from cold winds. Also, they resent root disturbance more than most plants and must be grown in pots. The best way is to raise the plants over a hotbed made in a frame at the end of March. Over the compost is placed 3 in. of fine soil and into this are pressed the small pots filled with John Innes sowing compost, but instead of peat incorporate some well-decayed manure.

Sow early March, pressing the seeds into the compost, their pointed ends uppermost and only just covered. Give them a thorough soaking and keep the frames closed until germination has taken place, watering only when necessary. To prevent the compost from drying out too quickly, press some damp peat around the pots when placed in the frame. During the first three weeks of April, cover the frames at night with sacking to retain warmth.

When the plants have formed their second pair of leaves which will be early May, they will be ready to move to a cold frame for hardening off. This is done by first leaving off the glass during the daytime, then gradually at night, so that by the end of the month the plants will be ready to transplant making room for other plants, or they may be grown-on in the open frames.

Planting and Soil Preparation

When manure was plentiful, one would see the marrow planted on mountains of compost, and how well they grew. Today it is a different matter for manure is scarce and in a warm dry summer which should suit them well, the plants make little growth. The reason is that the plants lack moisture, the little mounds drying out too quickly. This is fatal to the marrow for in summer it needs plenty of moisture at its roots.

With the present shortage of compost, the best method is to plant on the flat, into a soil containing plenty of humus – some decayed manure if obtainable, peat, spent hops, decayed leaves or bark fibre, garden compost or old mushroom compost, to help the soil retain moisture. If the soil is heavy or the ground low lying, make a raised bed, but it will need just as much humus.

Plant at the end of May, allowing 3-4 ft. for the bush varieties, and 6 ft. for the trailers. Where growing under barn cloches, make the beds to fit the cloches. The glass may be removed at the end of June, when the plants will have made plenty of growth.

If no frame is available, they may be grown entirely under cloches, and although the crop will not be so early to mature, it will prove earlier than where the seed is sown in the open. Plants sown over a hotbed will be showing fruit before seed sown in the open has made its second leaves.

Before removing the plant from the pot, give it a thorough watering to bind the roots so that there will be the minimum of root disturbance. Then transplant firmly into the ground and press the empty pot into the soil about 2 in. from the plant. Here, the plant is watered when the moisture will get down to the roots.

When the plants have made about 18 in. of growth, pinch out the leader shoots to encourage the formation of side shoots. Under glass give daily syringings to flowers and foliage when the weather is warm, and those growing in the open should be kept free from weeds and watered during dry weather. A mulch of peat and decayed manure will prove valuable as will regular watering with liquid manure from the time the first fruits begin to form. In the south, this will be about mid-July from early sown seed; about three weeks later in the north. Remove the fruits before they grow too large; courgettes when only about 4 in. long.

Summer marrows are harvested when the skin is soft (press in the thumb nail). If the skin is too hard, it will be too late! With winter varieties, the skin must be hard for them to keep well.

Care must be taken when removing the fruits not to damage the plants. Cut away the marrow where it lies rather than lifting first, for this will disturb the plant. At the same time remove any dead foliage. The large marrows especially should be handled with care so as not to cause bruising.

Pollinating Marrows

This is usually done by insects, especially during dry, sunny periods, more so in the south than in the north. However, the plants will begin to fruit earlier and bear more heavily if artificially pollinated.

This may be done in two ways; either by dusting the male flowers and transferring the pollen to those of the female; or by removing the male flower entirely, folding back its petals and pressing it into the female flower. This should be done only on a dry day, when the pollen is dry, and when the flowers are open and the pollen ripe. There should be no difficulty in telling which flower is the male and which the female, for the latter has a tiny miniature marrow-like swelling of the stem just beneath the flower. The male is without this swelling.

VARIETIES

The terms marrows, squashes, pumpkins, courgettes, mean the same thing, there being only slight botanical differences between each. Americans call all marrows squashes, those which should be used during summer straight from the plant, and those which will store through winter. They are amongst the most varied and valuable of all vegetables.

Avocadella. A summer marrow of bush habit bearing small fruit about the size of a large orange but deep green in colour. It is also known as the Argentine Marrow, and is popular in that country served cold, as it should be. After boiling for half an hour, cut in halves, remove the pulp and place in the refrigerator for an hour. Serve with the centres filled with whipped cream. Add sugar and a little oil, and if served at the beginning of a meal instead of soup or hors-d'oeuvre, it will prove a delicious appetiser during late summer and early autumn. The flesh is pale pink.

Banana Orange. Of trailing habit, the rich, orange-coloured flesh is firm and sweet, with the attractive flavour of ripe bananas, although it is on account of its long slightly curved shape that it takes its name. It will keep through winter.

Boston Pie Pumpkin. The old American pie-marrow, with orange skin and flesh. The fruits may weigh up to eight pounds. It is known as the Sugar Pumpkin on account of its sweetness. It is of trailing habit and, like most of the winter-keeping squashes and marrows, the fruits are never at their best until late autumn when they should be used with eggs, onions and other tasty winter vegetables. The Hubbard Squash is similar in all respects except that the skin is green.

Courgette. Also the Zucchini marrow, it is the French marrow, which should be harvested when only 4 in. long. This will ensure a succession of fruits which are cooked in their skins, frying them in butter or margarine, like sausages, when the skins will be just as tender, and slicing them afterwards, as one does a cucumber! They are ready to serve as soon as the skins are soft.

Gold Nugget. A delicious marrow of bush habit, each plant bearing six to eight fruits of deep golden yellow striped with white and of the size of a grapefruit. It may be used in summer and also stores well.

Moore's Cream. It may be used through autumn and, if carefully stored, into winter. A trailing variety, the fruits are small, oval and pale cream coloured. It is delicious baked in its skin which should be oiled, then with the pulp and seeds removed, fill with cooked tomatoes, beans and mushrooms, before re-heating in its skin and serving piping hot.

Patty Pan. A new F1 Hybrid of compact habit and bearing fruit of purest white, scallop shaped and yielding an immense crop if kept picked over the fruits and removed when about 3 in. across. Eaten raw or fried in butter to serve with meats, they are sweet and juicy.

Rotherside Orange. A little marrow of exceptional flavour, bearing fruits of grapefruit size and of similar colour. It is of trailing habit for summer use. After cooking, it is cooled in a refrigerator and served with sugar or ginger, adding cream or oil to taste.

Sutton's Superlative. A bush marrow, the fruits being bottle-green in colour, the flesh deep orange and very sweet. Though it will grow large the fruits are at their best when used small.

Sweet Dumpling. A handsome marrow, maturing in two months from planting, the fruits being large with prominent lobes which are shaded green, the rest of the marrow being white. The fruit is sweet and tender and it will keep through winter if stored in a frost-free room.

Table Dainty. The earliest marrow to fruit, and one of the most prolific. It is a summer marrow of trailing habit, the deep green fruits being striped with paler green. It may be used on its own or filled with chopped dwarf beans and tomatoes, served hot or cold.

CHAPTER NINE

FOOD FROM DARK PLACES

There are in almost all town houses a number of dark places which could be made productive. A cellar or garage is ideal for growing mushrooms in boxes or forcing rhubarb and seakale in winter. Because cellars are underground they are warm in winter, cool in summer, and so provide perfect mushroom growing conditions, a temperature of about 52°F. (11°C.) and the correct humidity. There will usually be space in the garage where boxes of mushrooms may be stacked around the sides so as to provide the maximum growing space, and if gentle warmth is already provided so that one's car will start with the minimum delay in the coldest weather whenever it is required to do so, conditions will be ideal to grow mushrooms.

There are other places too. Mushrooms may be grown in boxes under the stairs, or even beneath the kitchen sink, for contrary to popular belief it is not necessary to have them swimming in water. Far from it. All they require is sufficient moisture to promote spawn growth; in fact, too much water will kill the spawn.

The garden shed and the space underneath a greenhouse bench are useful places to force rhubarb, chicory and seakale, each of which, like the mushroom, prefers dark conditions. An old air-raid shelter is ideal for these crops. With Victorian town houses a separate wash-house of brick or stone was usually built. Now the washing machine has arrived to do the work of the old copper and tub. But what better place to grow mushrooms? The same may be said for old carriage-houses and tack-rooms, long since abandoned for their original purpose. Even if they have been taken over for the family limousine, with the high cost of petrol this may now be laid up.

Almost every house has at least some place to grow food and which is rarely put to any use. Indeed, many a specialist mushroom grower began in a cellar or outhouse with only a hundred square feet of bed space and found the crop so profitable that he (or she) was soon able to expand and to build up a profitable enterprise. I myself began mushroom growing in a large wine cellar and the adjoining coal cellar beneath an early Victorian house in one of our largest industrial cities, and soon had 50,000 sq. ft. under culture, supplying the wholesale markets throughout the north with some hundreds of pounds of mushrooms daily.

MUSHROOMS

Mushrooms grow better in the dark than in light simply because the beds dry out too quickly if sunlight reaches them, but total darkness is not essential and they will grow equally well in diffused light. If grown in a frame, cover the frame lights with sacking to exclude the sunlight; or if growing in a greenhouse, make up the beds under the bench and drape sacking down the sides. It is not advisable to grow mushrooms under glass during summer for hot, dry conditions are detrimental to a good crop. Mushrooms, however, may be grown under glass when the tomato crop has been cleared in early autumn. If the compost is made ready early in September, the beds can be made up at the end of October. Some slight heat will be necessary from that time onwards to maintain a temperature of 50°-52°F., (10°-11°C.) below which mushrooms will grow only slowly. Above 50°F., the beds will continue to crop until the end of winter, the greenhouse (or frame) being cleared early in spring for another tomato crop. Should the beds freeze up, mushrooms will appear again as soon as the weather becomes warmer.

Mushrooms always crop better in a brick or stone building such as a garage, cellar or barn. Not only is it dark, once any windows have been treated with limewash on the inside, but temperatures remain almost constant all the year, the building being cool in summer and frost-proof in winter, and if gentle warmth can be provided to maintain a temperature of not less than 50°F. during the colder months, the beds will be cropping when mushrooms are most required.

In all such unused buildings there should be mushroom beds ready to begin cropping by the end of September. This will mean preparing the compost during August. Early in the month, a load of straw manure should be obtained from a riding school, or several bales of wheat straw from a farmer just as soon as the first corn is harvested and the straw baled. This will be early in the month in southern England, two weeks later in the north. Wheat straw breaks down quickly and on it the spawn will 'run' better than on barley straw. Straw can be prepared in a cellar, and manure in a small yard or possibly at the end of the garden, but it should be prepared on a hard surface so that it does not come in contact with soil.

Preparing the Compost

When the wheat straw arrives, shake it out and make it into a heap, against a wall if possible, then add sufficient water to make it thoroughly moist – it is surprising how much straw will absorb before it becomes saturated. The preparation can now continue in the cellar, where this heap must be re-distributed.

Mark out a base about 5 ft. square and to these measurements place the straw to a depth of 15-18 in., then over the surface sprinkle an activator. This is a compost maker specially prepared for mushroom growing; Adco 'M' is long established and is obtainable from most sundries shops or from W. Darlington & Sons of Worthing, the spawn makers. Order it in plenty of time, for it will keep indefinitely , and use it to the instructions printed on the box.

If a small quantity of poultry or pigeon manure can be obtained in a dry condition, this will be invaluable in making up a good compost. It is clean to use with virtually no smell, and it will help the straw to heat up quickly and to a high temperature. Sprinkle the poultry manure over the surface with the activator and build up the heap in layers of about 8 in., adding the activator and poultry manure to each layer of straw. The higher the heap is made, the more heat will be generated, thus breaking down the straw more quickly.

After about nine to ten days, the heap is turned again, shaking it well out so as to mix the activator in with the straw, and add-ing more water if the straw appears to be dry. Then allow it to heat up for another week before turning it again. The straw will take about three weeks to prepare, at the end of which time it will have turned a deep brown colour with a mushroomy aroma, and will have begun to break down. When a handful is tightly squeezed, it should leave the hand moist, but excess moisture should not exude between the fingers. In other words, it should be damp but not wet. If it is too wet, the spawn will die, which is why a wet summer produces few mushrooms in the fields. The best crops always come in the autumn following a dry summer.

If the beds are to be made up on the floor of a cellar or out-house, the compost should be sufficiently moist to be trodden or beaten down with a spade to conserve its heat, but without becoming a wet, soggy mass as it cools down. A wet compost at this stage will deprive the growing spawn of the oxygen so necessary to promote vigorous mycelium growth.

Stable manure should be in fresh condition so that it can be prepared as above. Old farmyard manure which has been kept in the open for many months is ideal for growing vegetables but will never grow a good crop of mushrooms. A riding stable is the best place to obtain fresh supplies and they will often deliver for a small extra charge.

Stable manure is prepared exactly as above, except that only half the amount of Adco 'M' should be used. It should be dampened before turning begins, for the finished product should be in the same condition as described for a straw compost. Make sure that the horses are bedded on wheat straw and not peat or wood shavings. If straw is not normally used, most riding schools will use it if told of your requirements well in advance.

A word here should be said about the use of pink gypsum in the preparation of all types of mushroom compost. Its use revolutionized mushroom growing in the late 1930s, for if sprinkled about the compost in the same way as the activator, it prevents a compost becoming greasy and setting hard when cold, depriving the spawn of oxygen. Pink gypsum is obtained from builders' merchants and is not expensive. Use about fourteen pounds for a heap 5 ft. by 5 ft. high, or fifty-six pounds to a ton of stable manure. It is cheaper to buy it by the bag; it should be stored dry so that any not used can be kept for a later crop. It is clean and easily handled with no smell.

Those who do not wish to prepare their own compost may obtain a ready-made pack from Thompson & Morgan to place in a cupboard or beneath the kitchen sink when all that is required is gentle waterings to bring on the crop and keep it productive. The packs are made up of sterilized compost into which the spawn has already permeated.

Boxes

If the mushrooms are to be grown in wooden boxes, fish boxes obtained from Hull or Grimsby are strongly made and 6 in. deep, which is the required depth for the compost. If they are to be grown on the floor, the beds are made 3 ft. wide if against a wall, or 5-6 ft. if they can be reached from two sides, so that the mushrooms can be picked without treading on the beds. They are made 10 in. deep, which consolidates to 8 in. when beaten down. The compost should have a 'springy' feel about it.

Boxes or trays can be stacked around the sides of a cellar, shed or garage and if the boxes are 6 in. deep, this will allow room to water them and to pick the crop. Boxes may also be stacked in a

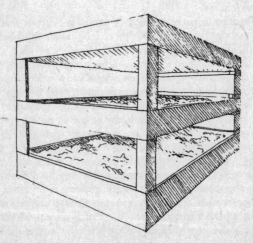

similar way at the centre of a room to form a rectangle, so that they may be tended from the outside. They can be stacked to any height, making full use of the room, and the top boxes can be tended by using a step-ladder. If there is no strong man to give a hand with the stacking, this may be done when the boxes are empty, but it is easier to fill them first and to stack afterwards in the manner shown in the diagram.

After filling the boxes, press down the compost around the sides especially, with a brick or piece of thick wood, otherwise the compost will dry out quickly at the edges. If the boxes are being treated with a wood preservative (e.g. Cuprinol) to extend their life, this must be done at least a month before they are used, to allow any fumes to escape which would be detrimental to the growing spawn.

As soon as the compost has reached the right condition, the boxes are filled without undue delay, though it may be necessary to do the work at a weekend when some help may be available.

Spawning

The spawn, too, should have been obtained in advance. Purchase dry spawn from a garden shop or direct from the makers. If stored at ordinary room temperature it will keep in active condition for at least a year. Moist spawn is only for the experienced grower for although it begins to grow more quickly than the dry, it requires that the compost be in exactly the right condition. A carton of pure culture spawn costs about 50p and is sufficient to plant about 50 sq. ft. Again, always use pure culture spawn rather than the so-called cheaper brick spawn, for pure culture spawn will have been produced under sterilized conditions and will be vigorous in its growth. If growing for one's own use, the brown variety produces a mushroom comparable in taste to the field mushroom, but for shop sale, the white variety is required; like brown and white bread, flavour does not come into it.

The temperature of the manure will fall to around 70°F. (21°C.) within twenty-four hours of the beds or boxes being made up. The commercial grower uses a hotbed thermometer to take an accurate reading, but no harm will be done to the spawn if the temperature rises again to 80°F. (27°C.) (which it sometimes does), so for the home grower a hotbed thermometer is hardly necessary.

The cylinder of spawn is broken up into pieces the size of a walnut; every particle of spawn is usable. Remove a small amount of compost with one hand and press in the spawn with the other, then replace the compost. It should be about 1 in. deep, no deeper, and it is planted 6 in. apart. Close planting will ensure that the compost becomes full of mycelium, the threads of running spawn, when the mushrooms will soon appear after casing. This is the term used for covering the surface of the beds. It is done about three weeks after spawning, by which time the spawn will appear at the surface of the compost as white circles or patches. This denotes that all is well. By now the compost will have subsided to about $\frac{3}{4}$ in. below the tops of the boxes, and this is the depth the casing should be.

It is most important to use sterilized soil to cover the compost. If not there is always the fear of introducing the dreaded mycogone disease, which causes the mushrooms to grow distorted and slimy and unfit to use. Never be persuaded to use anything but sterilized loam with which a little peat has been mixed. Most nurserymen have a soil sterilizer and will have the soil ready when you require it if told in time.

Do not make the casing too deep or the crop will be delayed, and do not over water the beds before the casing is in place. The casing should be fairly dry and be friable for ease in spreading. Make it level and firm by giving it a gentle tamping with a piece of wood. Then give it a very light watering with a fine-nozzle spray and if conditions are warm, do so again in two to three days, but never give so much water that it will percolate through the casing to the compost underneath. It is safer always to err on the side of dryness. Gentle syringing of the surface is more satisfactory than liberal waterings.

Care of the Crop

In two or three weeks after casing the beds, tiny pin-head mushrooms will appear, usually in circles, and slightly more moisture can then be given. About a week later the first mushrooms will be ready to pick. They are removed by gently twisting the base of the stem from the soil, taking care not to disturb those growing nearby which may not be ready to pick. Mushrooms come in flushes at intervals of about ten days. After clearing a flush, carefully fill in the holes with more of the sterilized soil and peat mixture so that the mycelium can grow into it again and more mushrooms will appear from the same place. A crop of about one pound per sq. ft. can be expected from the beds (or boxes) which, with mushrooms at 10-12p a quarter pound depending on season, will mean a handsome return on one's outlay whether they are used at home or sold to shops.

The beds will remain in bearing for three to four months in a temperature of 52°-55°C. (11°-15°C.). In higher temperatures they will finish quicker. An occasional watering with dilute salt water will usually extend the crop for several weeks. When cropping comes to an end, fresh compost should be ready to fill the boxes soon after they are emptied. Use the old compost for vegetable growing – it is ideal for this purpose – and wash the inside of the boxes with Ster-Izal.

The best time to make up the beds is early in autumn, for the spawn then receives enough natural warmth for it to get away to a good start; and again in spring for the same reason, although mushrooms are most wanted during the winter months.

The chief pests of the mushroom are phorid and sciarid flies, tiny midges whose grubs tunnel into the mushrooms, making them unfit to use. They are especially troublesome in summer but can be kept under control by dusting the beds each week with non-poisonous Black Arrow or derris powder.

Mushrooms in a Lawn

Why not make the lawn productive too, using it for its intended purpose, but also taking from it a crop of mushrooms in autumn? All that is necessary is to cut out squares of turf to the width of a spade and 2 in. deep. Then remove 4 in. of the soil beneath and in its place add some strawy manure, preferably from a riding stable. Beat it well down and into it press two pieces of spawn of walnut size. Then cover it with a little soil and replace the turf, treading it firmly down so that it is level with the surrounding lawn. This should be done in April, a time of gentle showers when the turves will knit together without delay and the spawn will have all summer to 'run'. If the rain is heavy, cover the sections of turf where the spawn is planted with pieces of plastic sheeting, removing them as soon as possible. This will prevent the spawn from being killed by excessive wet before it has begun to 'run'.

Pin-head mushrooms should appear late in August, after which the lawn should not be cut until the mushrooms finish about mid-October. At this time the grass will not grow long.

Watering where the mushrooms appear with dilute liquid manure or common salt will increase the crop. Mushrooms take about seven days to develop from the pin-head stage to a reasonable size for picking. Although mushrooms come up better after a dry summer, if the lawn is still dry by mid-August it should be watered well at least once each week to bring on the crop.

The spawn will produce mushrooms another year if it is not killed by heavy winter rains.

RHUBARB

This is one of the best of all crops, whether it is considered to be fruit or vegetable, to force in late winter and early spring. The succulent pink sticks are much enjoyed when the long-keeping apples are coming to an end and before the first of the new season's fruit crops appear.

Where it is intended to force the roots, no stems should be removed for two years. Provided applications of fertilizers, manure and peat mulches have been given each winter and spring to build up a sturdy root, the third season will show a good-sized clump which may then be semi- or cold-forced in early spring, or forced in heat the following winter.

Rhubarb may be cold-forced in a number of ways. Where it is intended to use lights, the roots are planted in beds rather than in rows. This will mean planting them closer, and having a path between each bed. Turf may be placed around the beds to add warmth, and to raise the glass so that the stems are allowed to develop to their correct length. Old bricks or stones are suitable but are less warm. The lights are placed over the beds, which are given exactly the same treatment as just described. To keep off bright light and to conserve as much warmth as possible, straw and sacks should be placed over the lights and held down by lengths of wood.

To force the roots in a building (and a cellar or stable is ideal) a quantity of hot well-rotted compost must be available to stimulate it into growth. This is prepared by rotting straw with an activator such as Adco 'M', and if a small quantity of dry poultry manure, some oak and beech leaves, and any available farmyard manure can be added to it, it will generate additional heat. The whole is turned several times until it is well decomposed. The compost should be ready for taking indoors early in February.

Outside, the roots are lifted and left exposed to the elements for two or three weeks. The more frosty the weather, the more they will benefit. Early in February the compost is spread out on the floor of the forcing room to a depth of 6 in. and several inches of soil placed on top. Into the soil the roots are placed close together, and a quantity of peat and soil is then placed around the clumps, filling in all cavities. The roots are given a thorough watering and all windows are darkened to encourage the stems to grow long and straight, and to be of a pale pink colour. The same procedure is used when the roots are forced in heat, only in this case the manure bed is generally dispensed with, the roots being taken indoors in December. It must be remembered that those roots intended for forcing would not have been pulled the previous summer or only lightly. Growth must be allowed to die down in the autumn before the dead leaves are cleared away, and the roots lifted early in December to weather.

Where semi-forcing in the open, if the roots are pulled only moderately and the pots or boxes used to cover the roots are removed after three to four weeks' pulling, the roots can be gently forced the following spring. There must however be no pulling the preceding summer. Give the roots a top dressing of decayed manure in autumn.

Those roots forced over a hotbed or in heat should be removed as soon as all pulling has ended, and replanted in beds which have been well replenished with manure and fertilizer. There they must be left for at least eighteen months, until they have recovered from their more severe forcing. No pulling should be done until such time as they have fully recovered.

Propagation

Rhubarb is increased by division of the crowns or by seed sowing, though a true stock may only be obtained by division.

The clumps are lifted in October and November, and the roots are cut into pieces, each containing an eye or bud. A three-year clump may be divided into as many as six or more offsets which are replanted into well manured ground.

The divisions are made with a sharp spade or knife; afterwards, dust them with hydrated lime to keep them as clean as possible. Provided that the bud is undamaged, even though there is virtually no root with it, the plant will grow in the spring, although it will take longer to build up into a sturdy forcing clump.

The raising of plants from seed will save money, but they will take three years to come into bearing and another year before they can be forced. The two most reliable varieties for the reproduction of seedling fruit are Myatt's Victoria and Glaskin's Perpetual. All varieties except The Sutton — a seedless variety — bear seed pods late in summer. Unless it is desired to save the seed, these must be cut off at ground level as soon as they form, in order to direct the strength used in the formation of seeds to the roots.

If the seed (which must not be more than two years old) is sown in boxes in a heated greenhouse or frame in September, the seedlings can be moved to the open ground in late March. Alternatively, sow seed direct into the frames in late March, or even into drills in the open ground. Provided that the seed is kept moist, it will readily germinate, and the plants will be large enough to transplant by June. They should then be planted in beds 1 ft. apart. The following spring every alternate plant is removed, and planted elsewhere. The ground must be well manured and thoroughly cleaned before the seedlings are transplanted. No pulling must be done the first two seasons, a little the third year, after which the roots will be ready to produce a crop, and be suitable for forcing, in their third year.

VARIETIES

Canada Red. A Canadian introduction excellent for cool forcing. The stalks grow large and thick and are a brilliant crimson colour.

Early Superb. An excellent new variety which is a heavy cropper, reaching maturity before Royal Albert. It forces well.

Red Sunshine. A new Australian variety, very early to mature and bearing large sticks of a rich crimson colour, sweeter than most rhubarbs. This, too, forces well.

Royal Albert. This is the best rhubarb for cool-forcing in the garden as it is hardy, very early and produces a stem of brightest scarlet.

The Sutton. One of the few rhubarbs to receive an Award of Merit. It forces well, and makes an immense stem of the most brilliant crimson. As it does not seed, it crops over a longer period than others.

Timperley Early. A fine new early of Cheshire origin. It forces well and bears long, stout stems of an excellent crimson colour when ripe.

SEAKALE

Like celery, this plant enjoys a deep, rich soil, preferably of a sandy nature but, provided that it is friable, almost any soil will do. Again like celery, the more robust the stems are the more tender it will be, so the aim must be to grow it well. It is a maritime plant and at its best growing in the salt-laden atmosphere of the coast. It must have salt in its diet, best given in the form of kainit, which has a high potash content yet contains thirty-three per cent salt. It is worked into the soil when the beds are being prepared in autumn at a strength of two ounces per sq. yd., and as much humus as possible should also be worked in for although the seakale enjoys a sandy soil it must have a supply of humus to maintain moisture.

Taking more than two years to mature from seed, seakale is usually grown from thongs which are sent out, tied in bundles, by specialist growers in early March. The thongs are removed from the main root before it is forced, the top of each being cut level, the bottom slanting, so that the bundles can be made up with each thong in the same direction. As the first roots are generally forced about the end of November, any thongs which have been removed should be bundled and placed in slightly damp sand, away from frost, where they remain until used in

March. Thus having once formed a bed, it should not be necessary to purchase more thongs.

Preparing the Soil

Make the bed 5 ft. wide to allow for hand weeding and lifting without damaging the plants. A slightly raised bed will prevent excess moisture remaining about the roots in periods of heavy rain. Then as soon as the soil has lost all traces of frost, towards the end of March, the thongs are planted with the straight end upwards. Space them 16 in. apart in the rows, with the top about 1 in. below soil level. Keep the hoe moving throughout summer, and never allow the plants to lack moisture. A peat mulch between the rows will be appreciated, and will suppress weeds, whilst an application of manure water once each week will help to build up a thick, sturdy root.

At the end of October, the foliage will begin to die down when it should be removed. The roots are then lifted and trimmed, and stored in damp sand in a shed or cellar, to be used for forcing when required.

Forcing the Roots

Complete darkness is essential so that the roots may be forced in deep boxes in a cellar or shed, in the manner later described for chicory, or in the open where indoor space is limited. Another method is to make up a small 'pit' against a garage wall which provides some shelter. On three sides, 3 ft. wide corrugated iron sheets are let into the ground to a depth of 8 in., and held in place with stakes. A small hotbed is then made up to a depth of 12 in. and covered with 6 in. of fine soil, into which the roots are planted 4 in. apart, keeping the crowns level with the surface. Water in and place some straw over the top. Heavy sacking is then placed over the bed to provide absolute darkness. Where there is a dark shed or outbuilding available, a similar bed should be made up indoors, where conditions would be better, being darker and warmer. A surround of bricks could be put in position to hold the bed together and maintain the heat of the compost.

The shoots will be ready for cutting in three to four weeks and when 8 in. long. After the roots have been forced they should be destroyed, a new bed being formed from the thongs which will have been removed before the roots are forced.

Lily White and Ivory White are similar varieties and satisfactory in every way, but whether they are tender and sweet depends upon how they are grown through the summer.

CHICORY

This is always expensive to buy but taking it right through from the time the seed is sown, no crop is easier to manage.

Early in June sow the seed in a rich soil. Do not sow earlier, or in a dry, hot summer the plants will run to seed. Sow in rows 18 in. apart, and thin out the plants to 10 in. in the rows. Being deep-rooting, a deeply dug bed into which some decayed compost and manure are dug in is necessary. During summer the plants must be kept free from weeds and comfortably moist.

Early in November, the foliage will have died down, and the roots – which by then will be about as thick as one's wrist – may be dug up with care, trimming off any small shoots, and forced. A cellar, cupboard, garden shed or barn are suitable places for this but some slight degree of warmth is desirable to bring on the shoots in about three weeks' time. One method is to fill a large orange box with freshly composted manure to a depth of 6 in. Over this is placed a 6 in. layer of fine loam and into it the roots are planted close together. Water thoroughly, and place in a dark room, or cover with sacking to exclude light. With the slight heat from the compost the shoots will be ready for use in a fortnight, being broken (snapped) off when 8-9 in. long, the roots being left to bear a second lot of shoots. If the roots are to be forced in a kitchen cupboard, the manure will not be necessary, but the other requirements will be the same.

Do not remove the shoots until required for cooking, for they require only a few minutes to prepare and when severed from the roots deteriorate quickly. The only variety to grow is Giant Witloof, which is tender and white when forced. It is delicious when cooked (braised) or grated raw in a winter salad.

CHAPTER TEN

FOODS TO GROW IN THE KITCHEN

In addition to pots of health-giving chives and parsley to be enjoyed green through winter in the kitchen window, there is also mustard and cress to sow all the year in pans of sterilized soil; or merely over a piece of moist flannel or felt placed in a seed tray, using no soil whatsoever. All that is necessary is to sow the seed thickly and in a temperature of 50°F. (10°C.) or more, it will germinate within three or four days and be ready to cut about a week later. But the cress, being slower to mature than mustard, should be sown four days earlier. A good idea is to sow half the felt with cress and half with mustard. The latter with its slight bitterness adds interest to a salad or to sandwiches, and the double or curled cress should be used, for it has a much richer flavour.

The commercial grower fills the bottoms of some thousands of punnets with a little sterilized soil and sows rape seed, which is cheaper and combines much of the flavour of mustard and cress. Whichever you use, keep it just nicely moist and cut it as required when about 2 in. tall, holding a bunch of top growth with the fingers of one hand and cutting near the base with the other hand. A fresh sowing should be made every fortnight throughout the year, anywhere in the home where there is light, a window or skylight or in a porch with a window. It may also be grown in a greenhouse or cold frame.

The growing shoots or sprouting seeds of a number of plants will require nothing more than the moist flannel or felt as used for mustard and cress. They do, however, require a higher temperature of not less than 65°F. (18°C.) and preferably slightly higher, the temperature of a centrally heated living room being suitable, where the seed can be kept in a sunny window. Most of one's friends will be fascinated by it, but if not, the flannel in the seed box may be moved to the kitchen for a day or longer with nothing more detrimental than the slowing down of growth.

ALFALFA, THE MIRACLE FOOD

One of the richest of all plant foods is alfalfa, its pale green 'sprouts' adding protein and its own particular flavour to winter salads. Alfalfa sprouts are fully digestible, photosynthesis releasing the protein, vitamins and mineral salts for the body to assimilate in the easiest way. It has forty per cent protein content and also contains every important vitamin, especially those of the B complex, whilst it is rich in salts of potassium, sodium, phosphorus and magnesium. Professor Cheeke at Oregon State University has discovered that alfalfa contains valuable cholesterol-reducing agents so that the plants may prove to be of the utmost importance in the prevention of heart disease.

A half-cupful of sprouted alfalfa seed contains as much vitamin C as six glasses of pure orange juice, whilst the vitamin B^2 value increases by more than one thousand per cent within four days of the seeds commencing to sprout. The chlorophyll content, too, is high and when it is included regularly in the diet, keeps the breath sweet and the digestive system functioning well. It is, in fact, nature's perfect food and can be made available all the year round by sowing the seed anywhere that it can receive light and warmth. It will be ready to eat within a week of the seed being sown and every day, in a temperature of 65°F. (18°C.) it doubles its weight so that when ready to use, it will have increased its weight ten-fold. If, after it has been growing for about a week, it is cut and placed in the coldest part of a refrigerator, it will keep fresh for many days; or it can be deep frozen. A good place to grow it is in the sunny window of one's office so that it may be used in sandwiches.

Sprouting the seed may be done in a jam jar or simply on flannel or felt and even in a saucer or dish with a piece of damp muslin over the top. Cover with water, then drain; the sprouting seed should be rinsed daily (twice a day is even better) and in five days it is ready to harvest. Cut off a handful at a time and use it in some way in the daily diet, when it will give the body a sense of well-being during winter time when fresh 'greens' are scarce. What is more, its flavour is like that of fresh garden peas and no vegetable is more delicious.

ADZUKI BEANS
Containing all the amino-acids and at least twenty-five per cent protein, they are used by the people of the Far East, where they grow naturally, like Mung beans. When sprouted, they are sweet and nutty, crunching when eaten. Grow in the same way as Mung beans and use the sprouts when just over 1 in. long.

MUNG BEANS (Bean Sprouts)
The Chinese or Mung bean may be sprouted where there is no light, as can many other seeds such as fenugreek and oats. The sprouts (not to be confused with Brussels sprouts) are rich in protein and especially in vitamin E, the food value of the sprouting seed being increased by at least six hundred per cent at almost one hundred hours after germination in a temperature of 60°F. (16°C.) It is at this point that the vitamins and their enzymes are at a peak.

The seeds (beans) are placed in a punnet or jar which has been lined with moistened flannel. Scatter the beans over the surface so that each is in contact with the moist flannel. Keep it moist and maintain the necessary warmth. After twenty-four hours, the beans will begin to sprout, increasing in vigour all the time; they will reach a peak of nutrition in about one hundred hours. Unlike alfalfa, the sprouts should be cooked before use.

FENUGREEK
Fenugreek has a spicy flavour and is often used with Mung bean sprouts. It is rich in choline, the natural fat-controlling factor, whilst it has internal healing qualities and so is recommended in the treatment of gastric ulcers. It contains thirty per cent protein and is rich in iron and vitamin A. It is delicious used raw in salads, though use it sparingly until accustomed to its spicy taste, and it is nourishing when included in soups and stews, to which it will impart something of an Eastern flavour associated with curries. Indeed, it was an important part of the diet of the people

of North Africa and the Near East thousands of years B.C.

It is not generally realized that sprouted oat seed contains almost twenty per cent protein and the important amino-acids, and is rich in vitamin E. The seeds are sprouted in the same way and can be added raw to breakfast cereals and to soups. They have a pleasing nutty flavour in salads. The seeds may be sprouted together with those of rye and millet for they will each germinate at the same time.

Pumpkin seed when sprouted is eaten by men of the Near East for, from earliest times, it was believed to preserve the prostate gland and male potency and correct urinary troubles. The sprouts are rich in iron and phosphorus and all the vitamins of the B complex, whilst they also contain thirty per cent protein.

Sprout the seed in the same way but use the sprouts when sixty to seventy hours old, either raw or cooked.

TRITICALE

It is a cereal grain and when sprouted is packed with vitamins and amino-acids. Like the other valuable plant foods for sprouting it was the Ipswich seed house of Thompson & Morgan who first drew our attention to its health-giving qualities. A natural cross between wheat and rye, it is sprouted in the same way as alfalfa and fenugreek, its sprouts being added to winter salads or used with cream cheese in brown bread sandwiches. It may also be sprinkled over the top of soups and stews. It is like eating freshly gathered runner beans.

INDEX

HYDROPONICS

Dudley Harris

PLANTS WITHOUT SOIL

* Labour-saving
* Virtually weed-free
* Gives bigger and better results

Growing plants without soil in mixtures of essential plant nutrients dissolved in water, is fast becoming popular with flower and vegetable growers everywhere. It is an easy and fascinating method from which flat-dwellers and householders with little or no soil, as well as farmers and commercial growers, can benefit.

In this practical and lucid handbook Dudley Harris explains the principles of hydroponics and describes the equipment necessary for its practice—from an ordinary window box to a concrete tank for the more ambitious grower. For beginners and more experienced gardeners alike, HYDROPONICS is an invaluable guide to a fascinating new dimension in gardening and agriculture.

0 7221 43400
GARDENING & AGRICULTURE   95p

GROWING, FREEZING & COOKING

Keith Mossman and Mary Norwak

A complete reference book for all who want the best results from their garden produce. It provides information on basic methods of gardening and freezing, and an alphabetical guide to many vegetables, herbs and fruits; under each heading will be found advice on cultivation and choice of varieties, followed by freezing recommendation and recipes for each product.

For all those households where gardening and cooking are regular activities, and for the ever-burgeoning ranks of freeze-owners, this book by two experts will prove invaluable.

0 7221 62545   GARDENING   85p

Mary Norwak has also written a book which presents a step-by-step guide for the complete beginner and a quick reference guide for the more experienced freezer owner.

There are notes on choosing and installing a freezer, what to put in it, how to choose and use packaging and how to avoid costly mistakes. HOME FREEZING: A BEGINNER'S GUIDE contains essential and useful information that will ensure that every beginner to home freezing soon becomes an expert.

0 7221 6445 9   DEEP FREEZING   60p

ON NEXT TO NOTHING

Thomas & Susan Hinde

With natural resources dwindling rapidly, supplies of many everyday items—from glass jars to razor blades to sugar—cannot last for ever. Prompted by current inflation and gloomy forecasts for the future, more and more people are looking for ways to maintain a comfortable living standard while spending less of their hard-earned money.

Thomas and Susan Hinde have been practising their own brand of self-help for years, and in this book they describe a wide range of practical economies, including preparing and preserving food, making anything from bread to furniture, and even tackling your own plumbing and house repairs. They prove that the pressures of modern living still allow room for a refreshing and down-to-earth code for low-budget survival.

"It brims over with ways of providing for yourself cheaply . . . precious money well spent"
Ideal Home

"Not a word is wasted in this excellent, down-to-earth handbook"
Sunday Telegraph

0 7221 4558 6   £1.25

NOUVEAU POOR

Barbara Griggs & Shirley Lowe
Foreword by Shirley Conran

LIVING WELL ON LESS

BUYING
How to keep those bills down to a minimum

ENTERTAINING
Impress your friends and still stay solvent

HOME
How to keep it looking good, all the time

GARDEN
The great money-saver

YOU
Looking stunningly up-to-date on a budget

CHILDREN
How to treat them without being mean

FREEZING
The great freezer myth

A FIVER
Fifty infallible ways to lose it

These are just samples of the fantastic wealth of hints and ideas on how to stay in style when money is scarce that can be found in this handbook for cheap living. It's a must for everyone who ever had to worry about money. And the chances are that means *you*!

0 7221 4081 9   REFERENCE/DOMESTIC   95p

All Sphere Books are available at your bookshop or newsagent, or can be ordered from the following address:
Sphere Books, Cash Sales Department,
P.O. Box 11, Falmouth, Cornwall.

Please send cheque or postal order (no currency), and allow 19p for postage and packing for the first book plus 9p per copy for each additional book ordered up to a maximum charge of 73p in U.K.

Customers in Eire and B.F.P.O. please allow 19p for postage and packing for the first book plus 9p per copy for the next 6 books, thereafter 3p per book.

Overseas customers please allow 20p for postage and packing for the first book and 10p per copy for each additional book.